GOLDENHEART II

WE ARE YOUR FAMILY

Editor & Author: Christina Goebel, M.A.

Co-Authors: BabyGo ♡ Kent Burles ♡ Jola Burnett ♡ Marcee Corn
Rob Corn ♡ Christine DeLillo ♡ Michał Domaszewicz ♡ Treasa Dovander
Dr. Shanni Dover ♡ Dale Driscoll ♡ Milton H. Elbogen ♡ Jason Francis
Neville Gaunt ♡ Peter Jones ♡ Michele Kelly ♡ Sema Küçük
Jill Magnussen ♡ Gerard McAlroy ♡ Joe Noya ♡ George Omondi Owiti
Kamla Peerbocus ♡ Guruji Gede Prama ♡ Amanda Ray ♡ Irene Reid
Kylie Riordan ♡ Angela (Lafontaine) Sarsons, M.A.
Todd Sarsons (Budokaizen) ♡ Rohit Sharma ♡ Jaana Uolamo
Pratosh Vashi ♡ Whitney Rix Victory II ♡ Dr. Jo Anne White ♡ Xue Wu
Helen Yu ♡ Noorio Zehra

GoldenHeart II: We Are Your Family by Christina Goebel, et al.

Edited by Christina Goebel.

Proofread by Joe Noya and Neville Gaunt.

christina@lovegoldenheart.com, www.lovegoldenheart.com

For information about educational needs or acquiring special copies of this book for orphans and foster children, contact christina@lovegoldenheart.com.

Printed in the U.S.A.

Visit the author's website at www.lovegoldenheart.com.

Published by Christina Goebel, Livingston, Texas
Edited by Christina Goebel
Proofread by Joe Noya and Neville Gaunt

Goebel, Christina, et al 2020 – GoldenHeart II: We Are Your Family

10 9 8 7 6 5 4 3 2 1

1. YOUNG ADULT NONFICTION / Family / Orphans & Foster Homes
2. YOUNG ADULT NONFICTION / Inspirational & Personal Growth
3. YOUNG ADULT NONFICTION / Boys & Men
4. YOUNG ADULT NONFICTION / Girls & Women

First Edition

Contents

Dedicated to the orphans, foster children, and foundlings of the world, and to every person who feels alone, has ever felt that way, or ever will. This book is for your heart, written especially for you, with you in mind, for you to keep next to your side always. Whenever you need us, we are here— forever. We are your family.

With love, the GoldenHearts

 In Memory of Pratosh Vashi

We called him #PreciousPratosh @pratoshnivedita

He lifted our spirits,
expanded our minds,
gave us laughs and adventures
of the most awesome kind.

"They all assume that if you have a successful career, a lovely wife and own a lavish residence, you're happy. However, not many are aware that true happiness is above all that. It comes from within. It's an inner feeling of gratification. Be happy friends. Truly happy."

Pratosh Vashi, tweet on August 6, 2019

Chapter One
We Are Your Family

Dear Reader, you are a special guest. We gathered our hearts here for you. Some people do not have parents their entire lives, while others of us live long enough to see our parents pass into another existence, leaving us orphans.

Almost all of humanity will spend time without parents. Most of us will be orphans one day if we are not now.

We are here for the world's orphans and foundlings, the people without a mother or father, as well as for the people who feel they have no one on their side, even though they have family. Relationships are not perfect, and we experience change, growing pains, and growth. If we are fortunate, we have someone to help us survive difficult times and we make the right choices to become our best selves and pursue our dreams.

We need people to show us understanding, encourage us, and have faith in us.

We understand and have been there, Dear One. We write from a variety of successful and painful backgrounds. As a group, we have lived through most of the things you will face. Between all of us, we have been orphans, entrepreneurs, leaders, managers, employees, writers, athletes, artists, musicians, students, teachers, businesspeople, nonprofit staff, volunteers, husbands, wives, mothers, fathers, children, advocates, and humanitarians.

Accounting for our combined experiences, we have been lonely, lost, homeless, beaten, abused, deserted, penniless, disabled, jobless, bereaved, and betrayed. During and after our painful experiences, we wondered what we would do and how we would continue. Having survived our difficult times and come together, we encourage you to continue trying, learning, and growing.

We believe in your precious heart, and that you will do well and make the right decisions to become your best self and create your dreams. People believed in us too—often strangers who became family—and we extend that blessing. Oh, Dearest Heart, we want you in our family—this one here, that speaks with you as often as you wish to read us!

We want two great things for you. First, that from now until the end of your life, you know that you are never alone and that we will always be here for you in these pages. Second, we would like to share anecdotes with you, little lessons like all parents share, with the hope that we can ease your decision making and reduce the time you spend dealing with the consequences of making poor decisions. It is okay to make mistakes and we all have, but they waste time and sometimes hurt, so we wish to help you avoid that.

The decisions you make will have the greatest impact on the quality of your life. If you are young, you have less freedom to determine your future, but it will not always be that way and over time, you will make more choices on your own. As we get older, people commonly feel that life is out of their control, and that others control our lives, but that is not true.

We always have choices about what we will or will not do and how we will do it. No one controls your mind and the thoughts in it. Only you.

In your mind here with us, our darling family member, you are powerful. You have dreams that no one else will dream. You can color your mind with beautiful thoughts worthy of kings and queens, Beloved. The things you think can make your mind more beautiful than a room full of jewels.

No matter what happens outside of your mind, or how dark life may temporarily become, inside your mind is your place and you decorate it how you want. We hope you will strive to appreciate life's gorgeousness. We will show you how we do it.

Because people who have not learned to love themselves are the loneliest, we will examine self-love first. Do you love yourself, Darling? Do you understand how a group of strangers wants to become your family? Do you realize that you are a one-of-a-kind, miraculous being with unlimited potential? Yes!

Every Olympic athlete was once a beginner, doubting his or her abilities. Thomas Edison widely publicized his failures before he was successful in inventing the lightbulb. Alexander Graham Bell was just another man before he invented a telephone and Henry Ford had no idea he was starting a legacy when he built his first car. Walt Disney did not know there would be a Walt Disney World or Disneyland when he drew the first Mickey Mouse. People used to write about going to the moon one day but did not believe it until they did in 1969. Oprah Winfrey did not know she would have a television network when she became a television show host.

Orphans have changed the world too, even when they became an orphan at a young age. You may have heard of Apple, Macs, iPods, iPhones, and iPads. Steve Jobs and Steve Wozniak started it all with Apple. Steve Jobs' mother put him up for adoption at birth and he was adopted by the Jobs family. One of the most famous actresses of all time, Marilyn Monroe, could not live with her mother as a child because her mother had mental illness and was in institutions. Famous musician and member of the Beatles, John Lennon, who wrote the beautiful song "Imagine," was raised during part of his childhood by his aunt and mainly taught himself to play the guitar.

When people realize who they are and achieve their true potential, they find their genius—their special gift to the world —and there is no limit to what they can do, because they will do more than anyone expects.

Your level of genius at what you are born to do is immeasurable—simply because YOU have never existed before, Dear One. No one knows your potential—not even you! You may not learn for years about your full abilities and so you must hold on, look, wait, and hope for the day your path is clear.

Try hard to find what you are good at doing and do it! But how can you do that? Try everything you can until you find it. Keep an open mind and willing hands and feet.

You will make mistakes, have some hard times, and feel lost, alone, and afraid. We will be here, wherever you keep *GoldenHeart II: We Are Your Family*, to help you restore the balance in your life and feel loved.

Welcome from Our Special Guests

All My Relations—We Are All One

It has taken me fifty years for life's lessons to penetrate my core so that I may be illuminated with the kiss of understanding. My gift to you is sharing the biggest lesson of all so that you may save time and step into the beauty that is you. It is simple, yet life changing—if you allow it.

We are all ONE. You are not alone, Little One; you never were. You might have felt alone, but you are a significant part of a magnificent whole. Does a leaf that falls silently to the ground cease to be a part of the tree? No, it will always be a part of the tree, no matter where the wind takes it, and you will always be a part of creation. It is a beautiful day when a wave realizes it is a part of the ocean.

I have been fortunate enough to be born into an Indigenous culture, one that understands the circle of life and the interconnectedness of all things. For the longest time, I wore the label of foster child. I pitied myself. I longed for my family to reunite. That day never came to be. When I started looking within instead of looking outside for the answers, I began to understand my perfection—not as an ideal, but as a truth. I could be still. I did not have to be or do anything to be a part of this glorious cosmos. The proof is my existence.

From this understanding, a deluge swept over me, and the outcome was a natural outpouring of deep gratitude for life. It finally dawned on me that I am LOVE, not I am loveable, since this quantifies love, but that I am the essence of love itself. Pure, unconditional, love. That is my birthright; this is your birthright. When you realize your self-worth, you step into your personal power. This is the essence of self-empowerment and no one can grant this other than you.

Now we can stand together at ground zero and start again. If you don't have a family, lucky you, you get to create one. They say that you can't choose your family, but you can always choose your friends. The world is filled with feuding family members who no longer speak to one another. In my experience, my friends have always been closer than family. Open your heart and give trust a chance. It may surprise you. Choose to nurture relationships that sustain you.

The day my marriage of twenty-four years ended, I was heartbroken. I felt vulnerable and utterly alone. I was on autopilot and found myself going for a walk while a stream of tears poured down my face. I had no regard for my surroundings or my safety. I just walked and cried. A car pulled alongside me. A man leaned out of his window and asked, "Are you alright, ma'am"? I said, "I'm not right now, but I will be," and thanked him for caring enough to stop. This is the moment I realized that people do care and it is up to me to be open and receive that.

No matter our lot in life, we have all experienced things that have changed our hardwiring and shaped the person we are today. That's OK. Many of us have been wounded by trauma and yet we survive. I am here to tell you that you can do more than survive. You can thrive! I marvel at how our bodies heal themselves and that through neuroplasticity, our brains can develop new neural pathways that change the trajectory of our lives.

Within each of us, a seed has been planted. It is our job to nurture it. What brings you energy? What makes your heart glow when you think about it? This is your special gift, the one the Creator bestowed upon you at birth. My Indigenous name is Wind That Helps Eagles Fly, given to me by a very respected elder. My special gift is that I am quickly able to see the strength and talents in others and I help to convey this. This love and encouragement has helped others to claim their purpose so they may shine on this earth. We are all here to serve and by doing so, we amplify the abundance that is ours. My brothers, my sisters, I wish you well in your journey and I want you to always remember that you are love and that we are all connected. All my relations.

© 2019 Angela (Lafontaine) Sarsons, M.A., "All My Relations—We Are All One"

Turning the Negative to Positive

I write to you, readers, these inspirational words to have a conversation with your hearts directly. Our hearts are connected through love. The Good Book says that love endures suffering, is patient and kind, and isn't jealous. It rejoices in goodness.

We are overwhelmed by loneliness as a result of frustration, rejection, pain, and the loss of our close friends, relatives, and families. You may have once undergone pain as a result of the death of a beloved one, which makes you an Orphan, even if your biological parents are alive. Today, it is impossible to find a family that has not lost at least a member. This makes us have a common relationship—we are all orphans on the planet.

Therefore, I expect to change the world through sharing what is in my heart and letting you know that we have the same feeling and you are not the only one who is finding it hard to survive. I hope to inspire you to let go of the pain that was already inflicted on you. There is always hope at the end of the tunnel, so never quit on your dreams. When you can dream it, then you can make it become a reality.

We are Your Family is the second GoldenHeart book, shared out of love to reach vulnerable families and orphans across the world. We therefore pass a light of hope to every orphan, foundling, foster child, or lonely person here.

Everyone can be inspired by these writings that will add value to your mindset concerning humanity.

When someone is advising you. and they don't know the exact nature of your challenges, they might give you strategies that worked for them that will not actually work for you, for the battles are not equal. Here, different writers who are orphans from around the world, and who have passed through the pain of losing parents or very close friends and relatives, have joined hands to share love and their experience with you, for you to overcome what seems complex in your life.

We can't control ailments, death, and hardships. We found

ourselves orphans and it made us feel broken, discouraged, afflicted, frustrated, and caused setbacks for us.

Many families are in pain from losing their loved ones, or have the huge responsibility of taking care of their ill parents, making life difficult for elder sisters, brothers and close relatives in the family when they have to meet various needs for the family such as education, food, clothing, housing, and medical expenses.

Many of us as orphans were once isolated and rejected in society, due to disability. Others were abandoned in hospitals and pits, left for dogs and wild animals to do away with us. I do not know what your story entails or your history, but I realize that history repeats itself. Someone is passing through the same challenges another person faced years ago.

When I was young, I saw my mother being beaten and teased by my uncles when they wanted to grab the land after my father's death. They were very snooty and aggressive in speech, but I couldn't do anything. My tears were the only inferior weapon I had then. My mother's illness became worse, eventually leading to her death.

No one could take care of her when her condition worsened. In two months, she was no more. What amazed me most is that people only contributed to her funeral arrangements. What I did not understand was if she was isolated because of HIV/AIDS—or because she was vulnerable? This has been a painful memory. I never trusted anyone from that day. I lost trust in men.

Despite the challenges I have faced—pain, frustration, rejection, and the loss of very important people in my life—I discovered that love still exists, and that I have a big family that is full of love. It didn't go with the deceased. I accepted who I was, believed that I have all it takes to change my thinking, and worked hard toward my progress.

If I made it, I believe you can make it too. Afflictions are there for moments, so never make a permanent decision based on temporary circumstances. The hearts of men and women and sons and daughters are filled with love and this you will only understand if you let go of negative thoughts and turn them to positive ones.

How will you turn the negative thoughts to positive ones? You find it very hard, don't you? That's the big reason we wrote for you what to expect in life, how to make changes, and how to be responsible in your journey.

We wish to install in you an awareness that you matter to many people in this beautiful world and that the decision you make today can impact it. It doesn't matter what you have. Being kind to someone, showing them love, and helping them make right decisions in life is much better than the treasures of this world.

An African proverb says, "The insect that is destroying the vegetable is in the vegetable." The only thing that can destroy you is yourself. Just as there are bad people among the friends you have and the relatives you know, there are also good people among them. Don't let bad people influence you with their poor character but keep being positive and joining hands with friends who are in support of the development of your positive character so that you leave a legacy of change. If you can make a positive decision out of the negativity and pain around you, then you win.

I wish to see your review concerning this book after you

read it. Remember, we are your family. We share the same pain and the same love. You are a light to the world and light only makes sense in the context of the darkness around it. Show wisdom and understanding by living a good life. As one of your family, I will be very happy with your success—seeing you serving humanity and working hard to uplift the suffering and dying souls. Wishing you the best of luck!

© 2019 George Omondi Owiti, "Turning the Negative to Positive"

There Is Light in Dark Times

Loved One, things will be very difficult at times, but it is at times like these where you need to look at yourself and love who you are. I was in one of the darkest places I would ever know; I had family and friends but felt very alone. I had depression and anxiety and at that time it was not really talked about. It was the most difficult time of my life, and at times I felt I could not go on; I no longer wanted to live on this planet. I broke down at my place of work and had to immediately go to the doctor to find out what was going on with me. Once the doctor told me that I was suffering with this condition, it was at that time I could move on and take very small steps forward, and from that point on I started to accept who I was.

For you, Loved One, things may appear bleak but there is always hope. You have a dream and you should never let go of that dream. The first thing you must do is accept that you are you. Everyone has imperfections and you should embrace those as part of who you are. Perfection is just an illusion, no matter what people tell you, or what they display on their social media, or the Internet—that is not the true extent of their life. You are you and the most important part of this is to accept who you are together with all your weaknesses and strengths.

When you look in the mirror, what do you think? The challenge here is to make yourself aware of your thoughts; remember your thoughts are not you, that is your mind and you are much greater than your mind. You have control over it. You can observe your thoughts, and let the ones go that do not serve you and believe the ones that lift you up. Just remember you are needed in this world. You are unique; you have special gifts and your purpose is to uncover those gifts and to show them and help the world be a better place. You are a miracle, Loved One, and this planet needs you and your gifts!

So, Loved One, how do we start to love ourselves and gain belief in ourselves? The first thing is to find out, what fills you up? What do you love doing? What is your dream? I want you to imagine your best life and display it somewhere in pictures or if you can, write out your most amazing life and how you want it to be. Start by becoming the person that is truly you; start by loving yourself and making space for the thing you love, then start doing it every day. Have belief that you will find a way no matter what.

Make a promise to yourself, that no matter what happens you are worthy and are needed, you matter, and you have a purpose to fulfill. You are perfect as you are, and you are going to use your strengths to build yourself into the best version of you, and no one and nothing will stop you, including your circumstances before being the person you want to become. This starts by every day, looking at the life you want, and day by day, by just taking just one action which moves you toward your dream. It's another step closer through your actions. Others will also start to believe that it's possible, and you will be a shining example to others. Remember you are LOVED, you are needed, and this planet needs you. Be you because you are UNIQUE.

© 2019 Joe Noya, "There Is Light in Dark Times"

Who Is This Person in the Mirror?

When you study yourself in the mirror, do you ever wonder who you are? The face looking back at you only reflects your outward appearance. It is the YOU that most others see and only a fraction of *all* of you. I want to focus on the more important piece of you; the part others may not see, the inner you, the more private you.

It is easy to describe the outer you: your hair color, height, skin tone, etc. But it is much harder to honestly describe your inner self. Think about the inner you for a moment. Then grab something you can write on or your phone and start your list. Let's start with something simple. Ready?

List six things you like. For example:

- I like chocolate milk.
- I love dogs.
- I like to play computer games.

Now list the things you don't like.

- I hate green beans.
- I don't like spiders.
- I don't like being alone.

Easy, right? And kinda fun.

The next part is a little more difficult. Make a list of what YOU are like, your personality. For instance:

- I am quiet.
- I am always smiling.
- I am sad.

The next one is hard. Ready? What are your passions?

Passions are described as things you feel **VERY** strongly about. A passion is a feeling of intense enthusiasm toward or compelling desire for someone or something. For example:

- I love to paint.
- I love John.
- I want to make a difference in the world.

Why do you think I want you to do this exercise, Dear One? I want you to think about YOU. Focus on the inner you because it is important. YOU are important.

Next, answer this question about everything on your list so far. Why?

- *Why* don't I like green beans?
- *Why* don't I like to be alone?
- *Why* do I want to change the world?
- *Why* do I love John?

The "why" questions require more time to think of your answers.

Your passions, likes and dislikes, along with your God-given talents, and a few other things make up who you are on the inside.

Finally, answer this question: what would you like to change about yourself?

While you can make certain changes to your outward appearance (haircut, hair color, new clothes), with work it is also possible to change your inner self. If there are things about you that you don't like, write them down and then write some steps that you could take to change those things. You can take baby steps at first. For instance, if you are shy and want to change that, write down ways that you can be more assertive. Example: I should say hello to three people at school or work that I don't really know well. Baby steps! The next day, make it five people.

We come into this world with an empty slate. And guess what? You get to write on that slate like a chalkboard. It is

YOUR slate. You can be whoever you want to be. With determination, guidance and pure hard work, you can achieve any goal you set for yourself. It is difficult to do. But it is important to start to think about the Inner YOU and to know why you are the way you are.

Did I mention that a slate could be erased? Yep, that is right. It can. You are a unique and precious soul but until the day you are no longer here, you are "a work in progress." Nothing about you is written in permanent ink. Erase the mistakes, forgive yourself and move forward.

Make your list. Change it when you want to or when it is necessary. Erase your mistakes and learn from them. Remember that YOU ARE a beautiful work in progress. Now, go back to the mirror. Look at your reflection there. I hope you smiled back. (Smile.)

© 2019 Marcee Corn, "Who Is This Person in the Mirror?"

Pivot toward Positivity

Choices.

We are all connected, yet all of us will need to find our own way, no matter where we started. For those who feel that they have led a life of privilege, had a rough start, have been shaken to the core by circumstances, or have lived through a continuous battle, know that things are not always as they seem and that all of us may be thrown off-kilter to different degrees.

During a period of my life, things went a bit haywire. I struggled to come to terms with some of the resentment, anger, hurt and guilt I harbored. I was stuck in a rut for sure and struggled under a cloud of underlying negative emotions.

Fortunately for me, something happened. I remember the exact time and place. It struck me that I didn't need to feel that way anymore. A sense of forgiveness came over me, and from that moment on, it felt as if a weight had been lifted. My attitude changed that day. I didn't need to hold on to toxic emotions. I could see the positive, even laugh, without diminishing the feelings of pain, anger, grief or sadness. I found a way to keep that inner light of love, trust, hopes and dreams flickering through gratitude. Wouldn't it be nice if we could extrapolate all the good energy from the universe and the stars above? Imagine filtering out all harmful things and keeping your light shining brightly. We only know that light by feeling love. We did not invent it. We experience it.

Having the support of people that believe in you is important, but it is necessary to believe in yourself. Not so easy to do. Since we are continuously learning, accepting and growing, the more you choose to see the positive, things simply become more "figure-out-able" and you need less validation from anyone else.

The more you give love; the more love comes back to you.

17

* * *

We all come to the realization that there can be a huge difference between other people's opinions of you and your work—and how you view things. Accepting and deciphering between being judged by others and constructive criticism can be tricky, but ultimately, no one has the right to judge you. If someone in your life, whether a parent, a friend or a stranger says, "You are a rare bird," then you take that to mean, "Yes! I am unique," and run with the positive implication. If someone says, "You are so predictable," then take that to mean, "Yes! I am consistent and trustworthy."

Sometimes, you need to think positively in the most difficult situations. I reference Jim Carrey in the classic movie *Dumb and Dumber*, when his character says, "So you're telling me there's a chance?" after he was told that the odds of going out with the girl that he adored were one in a million. (Spoiler alert: by the end of this movie, he gets the girl.)

Keep filling your heart with love, in any and all ways, since love exists wherever you find it. Know you are loved and love yourself.

© 2019 Christine DeLillo @VirtueValley1, "Pivot toward Positivity"

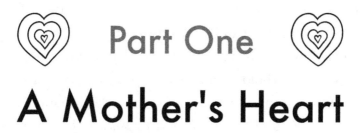

Part One

A Mother's Heart

Introducing the delight of the heart
of girls and women

(followed by A Father's Heart about
boys and men in Part II)

Beautiful You

Dear Sweet and Precious One,

I long for you to know a mother's love right now. My heart breaks for you that I cannot hold and comfort you in your pain and aloneness. Only you know the depths and intensity of feelings that you hold within. You have gone through so much and, at times, it must have felt like you've been shattered into a million pieces; and yet *you have come through. You are so strong!* Being strong doesn't mean that you never feel weak or powerless, but it means that you keep hanging on despite those times. It means that you keep rising every time you fall, and that you don't give up.

Would you let me *hold you* in your heart and mind right now? Would you allow yourself to *receive unconditional love* and *full acceptance* right now? Would you *listen* as I pour out my *Mother's Heart* to you?

I long for you to know and to feel my pride and delight in you just because you are my child—my beautiful child whom I love with all my heart. When I think of you, my heart is filled with joy that you are alive in this world. I know that *you are meant to be here* and that *you are needed here*. My deep desire for you is that you would *know* deep within your soul how *unique* and *special* you are; and that others will come to know your *inner beauty* too. I want you to experience a *life filled with purpose* and *rich in meaningful relationships*.

I'm so glad *I'm here in this moment with you*. I hope that you will always hear my voice speaking into your heart and *encouraging you* when you are down, *comforting you* when you are alone, *helping you* when you don't know what to do, and *reassuring you* that *YOU ARE ENOUGH, YOU ARE LOVED AND LOVEABLE, YOU ARE OF IMMENSE VALUE AND WORTH, YOU ARE WANTED*, and that, because of your uniqueness, *YOU ALONE FULFILL A PURPOSE THAT NO-ONE ELSE EVER COULD.*

I want you to know that the bond I have with you and the love I feel for you has nothing to do with your gender, looks or level of intelligence. My hopes for your future have nothing to do with your performance and achievements, or lack thereof. My love is for *WHO YOU ARE* rather than for WHAT YOU DO; and it will always be *total and unconditional.* I hope you can see, as I do, that you have an *amazing impact* on this world—just *by being beautiful YOU!*

© *2019 Jill Magnussen, "Beautiful You"*

Jack of All Trades

I AM an optician, to help you see
through your eyes filled with tears.

I AM a fortune teller, who gives your
hopes and dreams a future, through the years.

I AM a seamstress, to mend your clothes
and your heart that's broken in two.

I AM an eagle, with a sharp eye
who watches over you.

I AM a chef, adding a ladle of trust
and a cup full of tender-loving care.

I AM a builder, laying brick upon brick,
a wall to protect you if ever I'm not there.

I AM a nurse, to help you through a fever
and put a cloth to your brow.

I AM a teacher, to answer your questions,
the where, why and how.

I AM a magician, to wave a wand and
help chase your fears away.

I AM an author, with memories written
in my heart, and that's where they'll stay.

I AM all these things and more like so many others,
giving unconditional love aplenty, not an angel but a mother.

© 2019 Irene Reid, "Jack of All Trades"

Chapter Two
Making Friends

Dear Heart, we hope that you have some special friends, and if you do not, that is not a problem. Most healthy people have one or two good friends. Maintaining friendships takes time. Friends expect you to be there when they need you and they also want to spend quality time with you, so having too many friends can become a problem. We also have virtual friendships via the Internet and that is how many of us met to become part of your family.

An important lesson about making friends is that if you want a friend, be one. If you are waiting for someone to come say hello to you or invite you to sit with them at lunch, that is what you should do. Many people are concerned that if they start a conversation, then they will fail, or if they invite someone to sit with them, then that person may say no. We cannot live our lives in a pretend future of worry.

The potential disasters that run through your mind are make believe. They have not happened, and they may never occur. All we ask is that you try to be a friend—and see what happens.

While you are selecting friends, make sure they are people you want in your life and that you have some things in common that you enjoy doing. For example, if you like riding bicycles and playing video games, then a good friend might like to do one of those things. Since friends enjoy spending time doing things with you, if you do not have similar interests, then what will you do during your time together? Of course, you can learn from one another, but it helps if you have things in common.

The personality traits of your friends are important, Dear One. If you are selecting people you want to keep company with later, then they should be people who have a positive, accepting attitude toward you. If they do not accept who you are, then they are not friends. You should not have to change yourself to fit in with them. Select your friends and do not wait for people to choose you. They may not know you are interested.

We try new things with friends. If you like riding bicycles, you might like skateboarding too and a friend may introduce you to a new sport. However, friends should not expect negative things from you or things that make you feel uncomfortable. They should also not make you feel awful about yourself.

One of the hardest things about selecting companions is when you meet someone you like, but you learn that they have a bad habit you do not like or that their other friends are people you do not want to be around later. Many nice people may not be living an honest, clean, and healthy life. One day, they may change their habits and behavior, but you should not wait for that time. If they are a bully today and beat up others, then chances are that tomorrow, they may not be a new person. Allow the bully to grow up and stop hurting people and then be her or his friend.

When you make friends, especially when you are getting to know them, do not reveal too much about yourself. It is okay to discuss whatever you are doing. If you are in class together, talk about that, or if you play a sport, that is a good conversation starter. Save difficult stories from your life for when you know one another better. People enjoy positive talk, so talk about happy and fun things often and you will both feel good. You will see that people who say negative things every day have less friends because other people do not feel good around them.

Find people that you like and admire or want to be like one day and seek their friendship. Do not let self-talk in your mind tell you that they will not like you. Negative self-talk is useless. Keep good thoughts in your head and that will influence better things to happen.

If one person does not want to be your friend, then select another. Rarely, you will not have much choice in friends, and it may take a while to find some. During those times, we are here for you, Beloved, and more importantly, YOU are here for you.

No matter how many people you have in your life, you will have moments when you keep yourself company. Those are the times you develop your talents, enjoy hobbies and sports, and relax. Explore new things and work toward making your dreams come true. Many people in the world cherish and desire time alone with their thoughts, so when you have it, be thankful for the chance. And if you do not wish to be alone, then visit with us, your family. We are here, waiting for your return. We do not mind if you are early or late. With us, you are always on time.

Anecdotes

I'll Always Be There for You: Sorrow and Joy with Making Friends

My Darling, I hope you feel happy when I call your name intimately, though we've never met. In a way, I'm actually writing to my childhood self, a lonely little girl longing for love and friendship, who lost her father to a sudden illness when she was only eleven. I'm also writing to my beloved son, an only child, a precious little boy who has grown up to be almost a young man at sixteen in 2019. I thus feel free and honest to share with you a story of my and my son's struggles and victories with making friends.

I vividly remember the happy times when my father was still alive with a lot of friends. He was an orphan of war in the 1940s in China. He was adopted twice and didn't know who his real parents were. When he was about fifteen in 1949, his hometown was liberated by the Chinese People's Liberation Army. He worked as a security guard for the new local county government officials who treated him well—he was very grateful.

In a place not far from where my father lived, in 1948, one year before the founding of the People's Republic of China, my mother's father, a young army officer, was killed in a battlefield for his ideal to liberate China. A few years later, my mother and her little brother received government assistance, for which they are forever thankful.

A few years after that, my father and mother, both orphans of war, met, fell in love, and got married. As far as I can remember, they were both kind, grateful, and optimistic—I thought that was why they had a lot of family friends. But I didn't realize they could un-friend us until my father's early demise, due to sudden brain bleeding. At eleven, I couldn't understand why they turned their backs to us. I was disheartened, but learned they weren't real friends who vanished from our lives because my father wasn't useful to them anymore.

My mother grieved my father's early passing and our friends' betrayal. However, she maintained a few good friends who have remained faithful.

I'm thankful to my mother for having taught me how to gain friends: to be a good friend first! I still remember how I was rejected and humiliated in my middle and high school years by adults and kids when I tried to befriend them. But I tried hard to excel in my schoolwork and to be a friend first. I had thus gained some friends who are still my friends. With the same attitude, I've also made a few friends in my workplace as well as online, such as at Twitter.

When my husband and I decided to have only one child after our son's birth in 2003, we had both realized he might face loneliness and friendship issues in his life. We wanted to make sure he would make a few good friends like siblings. We were happy to see he was eager to befriend others in his childhood. One example has stuck in our memory.

When he was five and in kindergarten, he asked us to help him make twenty-five red, heart-shaped cards for all his classmates on Valentine's Day. He wrote a message on each card and attached a chocolate candy to it.

We were worried about his tendency to please everyone he had met during his elementary and middle school years. He ignored our advice to be selective about friends and thus experienced rejection and hurt. But we are happy he has gradually reduced his friends' circle in high school and is still kind and friendly to people around him.

So, my Darling, I hope you can learn both the sad and happy lessons from myself and my son in making friends and that you have or will have a few special friends who bring you joy, love, and comfort. Whenever you feel lonely, please read my letter and others in this book because they all have been written by some of my friends with love and best wishes for you and someone like you. We will always be here for you as your big pals!

© *2019 Xue Wu, "I'll Always Be There for You: Sorrow and Joy with Making Friends"*

The First Hi

"A *simple smile. That's the start of opening your heart and being compassionate to others.*"
the 14th Dalai Lama

You will find there are times in your life when you walk into a room or start a new school—where you realize you don't know anyone around you. Throughout your life, this will happen a lot, so it's a situation you should be prepared for and practice what you will do.

For example, think of your first summer job, your first day in university, a birthday party where you don't know many, or your first real job interview. You begin by feeling alone and unsure if people are friendly or not. You want to make an impression and make friends. Believe me, as a mom of three children and a friend of many; being brave enough to be the first to say "hi" is a life-long skill to master.

My advice to you if your heart starts thumping inside your chest and you are feeling nervous is simply to open with a warm smile. A smile says a thousand words in just a second and it shows you are open to having a conversation.

Sometimes, a good friendship takes a good few years to foster—you need to share the good and the tough times with a friendly listening ear. They need to get to know the "whole" you. They are the ones that can tap you on the back and say, "This isn't like you," or they will be the first ones to congratulate you when you achieve that first step toward your dreams—because you and they will have shared the most precious of secrets.

A word of warning: you may fall out at times with your friends. Different people part ways for various reasons—they move away, your interests differ or maybe they find a girlfriend or boyfriend. True friends may disappear from your life for a period, but how do you know if they are a true friend?

When they come back into your life it's like time stood still and you were not apart. I have a few friends like this, and when we meet up, we just laugh at the silly things we did, remember the fun times or talk about things we will do together in the future. It's as if they lived next door—even though they live thousands of miles away.

When I was young, I had several pen pals; they lived in different countries. I found that this was a great way to introduce yourself to each other and to stay in touch. Nowadays, there is Facebook, email and Instagram that make social communication quicker but perhaps shallower.

Take the time to get to know your friends, really know them—what they like, what they don't like, what memories impact them, what makes them happy, what they find funny and what they dream about. This will turn the conversation back to you—what do you like or dislike, etc. Be prepared to share, stay open and be a good listener. It's important if you are the shoulder to cry on later. You need to know the right things to say. You will only know this if you are a really good listener.

Make memories and events together special. Being with your friend should be easy, as if you are both swimming effortlessly together in the pool of conversation.

They say you choose your friends. I say choose wisely.

They will be the most precious gifts you will have throughout your life.

Countless days of laughter, fun times, football games and cinema trips together will be a well of inspiration for you. I promise these memories will overshadow any initial feelings of worry or concern you may have experienced when your heart was thumping, and you smiled to say your first "Hi."

© *2019 Treasa Dovander, "The First Hi"*

Chapter Three
Falling in Love

Dear One, love is one of the greatest things in the world. We can love many people as human beings, and this is admirable and right. We are here for serving others when they are weak or need assistance—or even to be nice—and the more we help other people, the happier we will be. We can also fall in love with someone special, someone we might like to date or marry.

Humans typically grow up, train for their future careers, find someone special, marry if they want, have children if they wish, and raise them. Because love with someone of the opposite sex is related to having children, we must be careful. When you love someone romantically, that is if you want them to become your boyfriend or girlfriend or more, and if you two do not become a permanent couple, it hurts. Many people say, "Breaking up is hard to do." And it is. For this reason, Beloved, you must spend time to learn about a person before you select her or him to be your loved one. You are trusting your heart with them and you hope they will be kind.

What is the purpose of love? Many people believe it is to have companionship, have children, and raise a family. True love feels like a completion of who you are and makes you want to be a better person. Love encourages you to do your best. A person who loves you will want the best for you, even if it is not the best for him or her. But each person is different and so it takes time for people to make compromises so that each person is happy in the relationship.

Jealousy is a common pain for some couples. This happens most when one of you has lost someone or felt betrayed before, so you are afraid to be hurt again. This pain can be bad for orphans and foundlings who are missing part of their family, so the new loved ones they have are extra special. People will do what they will, and we cannot stop it, but if we are compassionate and loving, we have a better chance that they will not disappoint us. Your mind may have many fears, but what you say out loud to someone you care about should be full of welcoming love.

What if the person you love does not love you back? This happens. Because you trust the person you love with your heart, you do not want to accept just anyone—especially someone who does not see how wonderful you are. You can be friends with this person and see if one day they come to know you enough to love you too. Since love is not forced, treat the other person with courtesy and kindness.

What if the other person has a loved one already, but they say they want to be with you one day? What hurts worse than a breakup is a breakup because of betrayal. If you begin a love relationship with this person, you would hurt someone else to do it. What goes around, comes around, so if you do bad things to others, then terrible things may happen to you as a result. Not only would you harm another person, but they could attempt do something to you for having a part in the destruction of their relationship.

If the person wants out of their relationship because it hurts, and they have tried to repair it and have failed, then tell them to end it as they have planned and to contact you after they have finished. This way, you are not involved in causing their loved one any trauma. We are not here to harm others. To do that feels wrong because it is.

Love is accepting, patient, kind, and forgiving. Love does not make you do what you do not feel comfortable doing. Love is not harmful or abusive. Love is not supposed to be violent or insulting. Sometimes, otherwise nice people make big mistakes in love that are not loving. When your relationship does not feel safe, reach out to others for assistance with counseling. These problems do not go away until they are discussed with others outside of the two of you. If the two of you could have solved the problem, you would have done that. Look online for free resources in your area for counseling or consult a leader in your house of worship.

Maybe you have fallen in love and someone has hurt you? For that pain, we give you a big hug. (((((HUG))))) The pain feels like it will last forever, Darling, but the pain will lessen. We have had our hearts broken too. (Frown.) We thought we had found the right person and breaking up was so painful that we wished we could escape it. The pain is in your head, though, so you cannot escape what is in your mind.

You can select which things occupy your mind and decide when you want to focus on something else. If you are spending most of your time being sad, then find an activity you can think about or do to give your mind peace. Some people read, meditate, watch television, play sports, clean the house, play video games, draw, or write. It may take you time to discover which things give you peace of mind, but keep looking, since this is a useful thing to know whenever you are upset about anything for the rest of your life. We all need fun things that we like to do!

To combat breakup distress, do what our parents or friends told us to do. Wait and be patient for the pain to lessen. Spend more time with friends. Watch funny movies. Work on hobbies. Journal about it. One day, you will not hurt so much and then you will be like us—a survivor. You cannot be a survivor unless you have lived through difficult times, so when you have, you join the rest of us as a stronger person.

While another person may complete you, that does not mean you must have a love interest. Our purpose is to love, help, and serve the world, not just one person. In fact, if you do kind things for others while you suffer, you will fulfill your purpose and feel better than when you only think about yourself. Like we reach out to you, Darling, spend time being there for others in need.

 # Anecdotes

Tipping, Tripping, Falling in Love

My Dearest, when we are very little, almost all of us dream of falling in love. It is a grand dream! Many of these thoughts are shaped by fairytales where two people meet—very often two people from different backgrounds—and find in each other something they are missing inside themselves.

While fairy tales are made-up stories to entertain, I do

believe in this basic truth of falling in love with someone who has a superpower we ourselves may not have.

Take heart if you have not fallen in love yet. Do not be scared if you have. Falling in love creates a much broader awareness of yourself. It is scary sometimes because we can fall in love and not have that love returned. When this happens, you must feel my arms around you in a big bear hug! Because as your heart breaks, so will mine. Let me tell you about the other kind of falling in love, my Dear One, the kind that is returned and is once and forever.

Falling in love with THE one happens when the other person fits, like a puzzle piece, right in the empty spot in your heart, a place longing to be filled.

You might wonder: how do I know if someone is the right person for me? Let me tell you a story about myself and you will see.

When I met my husband, Roderick, he made me laugh the first time we talked. We met in business. I had a public relations firm and he was an editor at a news service agency. I pitched a story to him. Since I'm always late for things (are you that way too? It just means we are busy people accomplishing many things! :), I was late the day we met at my client's office. While I cleared the first set of glass doors, I didn't see the second set and face planted right onto the glass! He told me that I looked like a bird hitting a window. I laughed uproariously, even though my head was throbbing. That night, I couldn't help but think how wonderful it would be to share a life with someone who looked at things with calm and humor. We married eight months after our first date.

It wasn't just his humor; it was also his values. In this

dialogue between you and me that is rooted in all the love and openness of heart one can have, know that falling in love means falling in love with another person's values. This is where the intimate story I am sharing with you continues.

I liked Roderick so much that I decided to ask him on a date (for all the girls reading this, be confident about pursuing what you want in life; you have everything it takes to achieve your dreams if you just go after them with a smile and confidence).

He declined.

You might be surprised to hear that because he had no girlfriend and was very attracted to me. The reason he declined was because the article he was writing wasn't yet published. He would not engage on a personal level with an interview source until a story had run. His values came through his actions.

My role as someone who cares deeply about you is to arm you with advice that will fortify your life journey, so as you grow and meet people who are super cute, fun, attractive in all the ways that move your heart this way and that, you regard love in good and healthy ways. Ask yourself these questions: Do we share the same values? Does he/she make me feel whole? Do I make her/him feel whole? Are we stronger together? If I had to go into battle, would I want this person beside me? Does holding his/her hand give me comfort, the kind you get from a plush blanket on a cold winter's night when summer seems a thousand days away?

It isn't always love at first sight, boom, you're done. Keep in mind I had thought I was in love before. Most people do fall in love multiple times. It's the one that sticks, the one you feel you do not want to live without who becomes THE one. Sometimes, love starts out as friendship or as a friend of a friend. Eventually, love winnows its way like a string from one person's heart to another, connecting them until they find that the best of life is with one another.

I believe, too, that love changes over time. Early on, there is the love of attraction, a physical love that is natural between two people. Love grows and you see how the other person reacts to things, how they support you, and in what ways they overcome problems. If you decide to marry on the heels of all this, love takes a different face. Love may not seem as exciting as it once was, but, tell me, Darling, does your oldest sweatshirt, the one that you fall into and hug yourself with because it's so soft and worn, look as new and crisp as it once did? It does not. Yet, you are so grateful for its warmth and comfort. This is happily ever after love.

Lastly, commitment is the other side of falling in love. You deserve the best; this I know. Never compromise when it comes to love. The other person should not love you "well enough." He or she should love you for who you are and every part of you. Have faith in that other person and open your heart to allow them to have faith in you. Falling in love is like hockey— a player slides the puck to where they know their teammate will stand, but the teammate is not yet there. The other person will have your back and you will have theirs. And each time this happens, you fall in love.

Again, and again and again.

© 2019 Michele Kelly, "Tipping, Tripping, Falling in Love"

Love Wins

When I ask myself
what love is,
the answer is—the light inside.
It's your soul's blessing.
It's your heart's prayers.

Reach into your divine well.
Your life will go into duels,
but you are not alone.
Your happiness won't be long postponed.

I say to you, Beautiful Being,
this is the challenge of forgiving:
be only kind.
Your heart will not mind.

Give whatever you can.
All the Divine's creatures will be your fan.
Do your best, so the sunset will never come;
so there will always be sunrise in your life—
and your love will thrive.

© 2019 Sema Küçük, "Love Wins"

Chapter Four
Communication

This is for girls and women who want to understand women and for boys and men who want to understand women. You may ask why women want to understand women. Our whole lives, we will define and redefine ourselves. We are different from everyone else who is a woman or a man. However, there are common things women face and challenges women overcome. Later, in the section for A Father's Heart, we will share ways to understand men.

A woman is not someone who wears a certain type of clothes or has one type of habit. While some women wear dresses and love glitter nail polish, others ride horses, work on cars, or do not wear makeup. Do what you are born to do, and if you do something well, so long as it is within the law and appropriate, then do it. How do we know if a woman is supposed to work on cars? Is she interested and able? If yes, then maybe she is supposed to repair or build cars. Otherwise, why does she have this gift?

Women have similar challenges across the world that affect how they feel and behave. There are things that women cannot easily do without disapproval or breaking a law. Women may earn less money than men, even though they may be the family worker who brings home paychecks to provide for the family. For example, until recently, women in Saudi

Arabia could not drive a car. Society had to see the importance for women driving and then the law was changed. Of course, some women said something about it so that people investigated what could be done.

One large difference between men and women is that women can give birth to children. Children need many things, and multiple children need different things at the same time, which is why women may be comfortable doing more things at once than men. Babies have difficulty communicating before they learn to speak, so this may be why women tend to be good with conversation clues and understanding what others say.

According to experts, women are raised to discuss their problems with others, and men are taught to solve problems by themselves. When women do not feel that they are free to talk about solutions they are attempting to find for their challenges, then they may feel unaccepted or become depressed. The way to improve communication with most women is to listen to what they say well enough that you may comment upon it. A woman does not need you to solve her problems when she shares them. She may be thinking out loud only to hear her thoughts and see if you agree with her logic.

Naturally, if a woman shares personal information with you, that means that she values your input. You do not need to agree with her position. All she requires is that you understand what she is thinking, and you will let her know that by responding to her with some comment.

For example, if a woman says, "I am having problems with my friend, Sarah. I think she is jealous of me," something you could say to show that you understand is, "What makes you think she is jealous of you?" Continue through the conversation trying to comprehend the situation. Our whole lives, we are students learning about people. Asking questions in conversations helps us to know more.

Though women give birth to children, that does not mean that they will act a certain way or be a devoted mother. Do you know that even some animal mothers do not care for their babies well? Many female dogs are great mothers, and some are not. So, this is not limited to people.

Each woman is different and has experienced a variety of situations, good or bad. Women who live alone are more likely to live in poverty, for example. They cannot work in just any job and in many cases, there are occupations for which not many women work, such as for the construction of buildings or roads. Let us not put expectations on people for the way they are formed. It causes much offense and anger.

Another thing that many women have in common is that they often have been encouraged to share their emotions with other women from a young age. Science tells us that women's brains work differently than men's do, in that they access their emotions easily. Sometimes, it is a challenge for women to manage these open emotions. If you see an upset woman, demonstrate your desire to understand her. Talking over her may make the problem worse.

Beloved, listening is a beautiful talent that will improve your relationships with everyone. Speaking teaches us about ourselves but listening teaches us about the world.

Anecdotes

The Chatterbox

Women love to talk. Women *need* to talk! While men like to give the main headlines of their day or of an event, women love to fill in all the juicy details and make it come to life! Much like a coloring-in book, men draw the outlines but it's women who color it in their own way—sometimes using strong and bold colors and other times soft and soothing pastels.

When my husband and I were dating, I once described to him a movie I'd seen that day. He was taking me out to dinner that night and afterwards driving me to his parents' house thirty minutes away. Well, I started telling him about the movie at the beginning of our meal and I didn't finish until we arrived at his parents' house. He said afterwards that he would never have to watch that movie since he feels like he's seen it already. He still remembers more about it than I do thirty-five years later!

My husband had to build his capacity to *actively* listen to me. In our early years of marriage, I would want to discuss something with him to the nth degree and after a while he'd get this glazed look in his eyes that told me he'd reached his limit. I'd find this so frustrating and I thought it meant that he didn't really care. But I came to learn that he was feeling overwhelmed and helpless because he thought I wanted him to do something about the situation and solve it for me, but I just needed him to listen and be there.

While men might be detailed in capturing the *facts* of a

happening, women notice all the *feelings* involved. If my husband went to an event or meeting that I was interested in without me, I would make him describe everything that was said from the very start and would often go back to him to extract more details until I was completely satisfied that I had all the information—not just the facts, mind you. I wanted all the nuances of the conversation, including the facial expressions, body language and the emotions expressed or unexpressed.

After a while, I realized that I put too much pressure on him to see things about which, frankly, he was oblivious. It's better to ask a woman if you want that sort of detail or to go yourself!

Because only women can really understand women, it's important for females to have female friends. I love getting together with women and chatting over a coffee. This gives us a chance to exchange all the *emotions* that we are experiencing, along with the details. Talking through our experiences is like letting out a pressure valve or unclogging a blocked drain in our *emotional tanks*. The best sort of friendships are with women who not only unload on you, but with whom you can unload. This is a great balance for us as women because we need to get things off our chests, but we also need to nurture and care for others. You'll know this type of friendship because you'll *both* feel refreshed and light after you've spent time together, rather than drained and heavy.

© 2019 Jill Magnussen, "The Chatterbox"

Chapter Five
Preparing for Work with Soft Skills

Most people work one day. They may work from home or in an office, or at a store or another location. Even people who do not work for money clean their homes or complete volunteer activities. Doing things that other people value makes people feel better. It gives us a sense of worth and belonging. We discussed your gifts earlier, Beloved, and how we would like you to watch for things you do well so that you will fulfill your greatest work and contribute to the world as only you may do one day.

When you are old enough, you will work if you do not already have a career. For some, it takes a lifetime to learn that completing tasks is only part of a job. If you work every day and do the things that they ask you to do, that is not all that is required to be successful. If a leader asks you to do something, and you say, "No, I don't feel like it!" then probably you will fail or be fired. The skills related to your behavior at work are called soft skills. While you may study about employment at school, college, or elsewhere, the soft skills are not taught as often—though they are needed to have work satisfaction.

If you are young, then completing chores or schoolwork is work. A successful student or businessperson have many things in common. They complete their work, maintain strong relationships with their leaders and teams, respect authority, and act appropriately. They develop skills that ensure that they receive better grades, rewards, awards, or pay. People who master soft skills well are often treated with more respect. We wish you to be respected always, so acquiring soft skills is a worthy goal.

Maybe you have thought that some people are loved more for no reason? This is not usually true. Some people act in a way that is easier to accept. If a person smiles and says hello to you every day, then you will feel better about him or her than someone who never speaks to you or smiles. The soft skills help others appreciate what you have to offer.

The soft skills we will focus on here for school or work are:

- Work Ethic
- Handling Change
- Teamwork
- Leadership

Work ethic

Before you go to school or for a job interview, prepare to demonstrate that you will be professional. Dress appropriately, usually in the clothing that they wear at that location. People wear clean, unwrinkled, and professional clothing to interviews. Even if you have little money, be resourceful. You can perhaps borrow a nice outfit from a friend. Your clothes should not show off your body, but prove you are there to complete tasks and not be a distraction.

Plan to wake up early on interview day or for school. Lay

out your clothes the night before and when you set your alarm, allow yourself more time than you think you will need. If you have difficulty waking up, set more than one alarm or even borrow a loud alarm clock. Arrange your transportation ahead of time and plan the times it will take you to arrive there, including traffic or potential delays. If you must be late for an interview, call them. In a nice folder, take a copy of your professionally typed resume with you in case the interviewer didn't print it. If you are a student, bring the required supplies.

Once you are at school or are hired at work, demonstrate that you are a reliable student, employee, or leader. Read all the information they give you. Learn your schedule, transportation needs, how to call in sick or request personal days or vacation (if you will have any of those), and how they would like you to handle any conflicts or problems.

As a new student or employee, observe and learn. Do not criticize systems, students, or employees. Give yourself weeks or a month before you determine if you know enough to propose changes. Keep your workspace neat and organized, including filing desktop documents. Clean up after yourself, including wiping up any messes you make in shared kitchen areas.

Work during the times you are expected and take breaks as scheduled. Return from lunch or breaks on time. Teachers or management will watch your behaviors to see that you are on time, organized, do not call in sick or for personal days at the last minute or against policy, work consistently throughout the day, and that you are easy to instruct without giving them hassles. If you are caught doing something that you should not have done, accept their reprimand or documentation without complaining, do not use a harsh voice or angry expression with them, tell them that it will not happen again—and make sure that is true. Arguing with leaders is a fast way to lose their respect and be forced to leave a job or school.

Handling change

Handling change is a vital career skill. Things will not always go as planned. Sometimes other businesses or people will impact your team's schedule or workload. Leaders or business owners may change their mind at the last minute. Other people may suddenly leave. Systems may fail.

We all have problems at work or school and what makes us a valuable employee, student, and team member is that we adjust, propose solutions, and move forward. If we complain, then we lower the team morale and may slow down the team. We may also make leadership think we are not worth the trouble to keep. Provide creative solutions to change. Try not to let your emotions interfere with progress.

Teamwork

If you have a great relationship with your teacher or supervisors, but do not get along with others, then you will have problems. Whether a teacher or supervisor, leaders must ensure that everyone gets along. If someone frustrates or makes others angry, then the leader will reprimand that person or remove him or her. People who work well with everyone are desired and those who make people feel uncomfortable are not. You do not have to be like everyone else. No, Beloved, you are one of a kind! You are also one who should be kind to everyone, even if they are different from you in ways that bother you.

Teams desire a few things. We should listen to everyone's ideas and give useful and respectful feedback. They want us to tolerate those things that we do not like and find solutions for problems rather than complain. Team members hope that if you have a problem with them that you will speak with them first before telling a supervisor or teacher—unless they have broken policies there and you are required to let leaders know.

If someone is sick, late, or having a problem, team members hope that you will show concern and speak to them with care and understanding. Some people will work quickly and some slowly. Some will need help and others will be ahead of you. You may work with men or women, or people of different ages, religions, or races. Whatever their situation, teams hope that you will be patient with their different ways. If people do not get along, gossiping about team members makes enemies.

Do not speak unkind words about others, even when everyone else is. Otherwise, people will think that you will gossip about them one day too. Assist others in making peace with one another. Most people appreciate it when you can say funny things, so see if your team enjoys a sense of humor from you. Being funny can relieve tension and make people feel more comfortable. Learn when telling jokes is not appropriate, too. Do not tell jokes that may offend people who are different. Comedy should not divide people and make them feel unwanted.

If you get along with your team but do not complete your

work, then they will not want to work with you. Each team member needs to complete her or his own assignment. Rather than criticize people who do not move along as quickly as you, offer to assist them and see if you can teach them what they need to do to improve. If you are behind, ask for help from team members or leaders before the problem gets out of control. If you cannot complete a task, give everyone advanced notice. If your team must plan times to work together, try to rotate times or places so that they do not benefit one person only.

Communicate with team members working on the same project about your progress and any delays. Do not surprise them with bad news or give them a ton of information at the last minute. Keep them informed as you work so that communication is comfortable. Work with each team member's communication style. Some prefer the phone or texting, while others want to receive emails. If everyone has a lot of information to exchange, suggest meetings and limit them to the amount of time everyone agreed to beforehand. Ensure that each team member has time to share.

When you disagree with others, one way to do that is to have an argument. That conflict may destroy your relationship with that person, other team members, management, customers, and others.

The other way to disagree is to use diplomacy to reach solutions that are a win for everyone. Listen to the other person's complaints and respond with understanding. Explain the reasons behind your point of view and do not expect others to automatically understand you. They will not know what you are thinking. You are one of a kind! (We are too, and they are too!) If the other person cannot calm down enough to communicate or if they start name calling, then request communication assistance or mediation from a leader.

You do not have to win against your teammates, Dear Heart. No. You are part of a team accomplishing a job together. If only you win, then the team loses. All you must do is understand one another and continue with your duty. You do not have to agree so long as you can continue what you were doing without having more problems. If you cannot do that, then either you do not understand one another and need to explain a different way so that they finally get what you are saying, or you may need a person to assist you with that understanding, a mediator.

If the other person is abusive, follow your leader's policies to file a complaint. Leaders hope that you will resolve as many problems as you can without running to them; however, there may be times when you need the leader's help. If you are uncertain, ask your leader.

Leadership

Every teacher and employer wishes to find leaders: helpful people who unite teams and help people accomplish more in less time with fewer problems. Leaders are not just people who order others to do things. In fact, they should not be forcing anyone to complete tasks. They should be motivating others.

Leaders are often selfless. To be selfless means that the leader works toward meeting team goals without a concern about what they will personally get out of the activity or doing it their way with no exceptions. They share a vision that benefits the team. They give others the information or tools they need to perform well. They want projects completed the best way and realize that someone else in their group may have the superior idea.

Leaders will ideally think less of themselves and more of the school, business, or team. Their goal is not to be better than everyone, but to help everyone be better. They realize that the team goal may not be the most important thing in everyone's lives. Their teammates may want to be playing sports or painting instead, but they have projects to complete as a team.

A leader listens to teammates, even when they talk about things that seem unimportant, so they may learn about the talents of each person. They also try to understand each person's culture and what makes her or him different and what motivates each one. Once a leader learns what each person does best and what motivates them, then the leader can better help organize projects using each person's skills at his or her best. Teams who feel understood support their leaders because they are leading.

 # Anecdotes

Leading with Soft Skills

Hello, my dear. As you may be thinking about the world of work, below are a few important characteristics that can help you stand out and succeed. There are two types of skills in the workplace: hard skills (such as math, coding or writing) and soft skills. Soft skills are those intangible qualities that can help you improve your work performance. Sometimes, people have similar hard skills. Having your soft skills shine can help a manager make the decision to hire or promote you over another candidate. Here are examples of soft skills:

- Confidence & positive attitude,
- Work ethic,
- Time management,
- Being a team player,
- Empathy, and
- Accepting feedback & finding a mentor.

Confidence & positive attitude

You can beautifully intertwine these two soft skills to make you shine, so let us talk about them together. When it comes to confidence, let me start by sharing one of my favorite quotes with you (from *Pooh's Grand Adventure: The Search for Christopher Robin*), "You are braver than you believe, stronger than you seem, and smarter than you think." Please do not let anybody ever let you think otherwise. Be confident in your abilities, sweet darling. No one is born an expert. No one who starts their first job knows everything—and some perceive the "know-it-alls" as arrogant anyway. Be humble, confident, curious and eager to learn.

Some jobs we start with are not what we really want to be doing in the end; yet, each work experience can teach us important skills and lessons along the way. Please keep your eyes on the goal. Despite other challenges you may be experiencing, try to keep a positive attitude. Sometimes, we just need to put one foot over another to keep moving. The combination of a positive attitude, confidence and hard work can help you succeed. Finally, if you have the tendency to say you are sorry every two minutes, please refrain from it. You do not have to apologize for your existence, my darling. Only apologize for things that you genuinely regret. Saying you are sorry will not help you appear confident, so shush the "sorry."

Work ethic

Another very important soft skill is work ethic. This means being diligent and giving your best effort at work or school. Regardless of what you do, even if it is a temporary job, pay attention to details and always give your best. Sometimes, this means giving your extra effort to complete something.

After completing a task, look back and ask yourself, "Was this my best work? Was there anything else I could do?" If the answer is "Yes, I could have done better," then it means maybe you did not give your 100 percent. If the answer is "No, I gave my absolute best and there was nothing else I could do better," then you can sleep soundly knowing you did everything you could to do your best work.

With that said, my dear, always strive for excellence, live with "no ifs" and challenge yourself to grow. Look back at your last assignment and see how you could improve upon it, or what else could you do to accomplish it more efficiently. If you ever fail, learn a lesson from it and move on. Do not dwell on it or let it drag you down.

Time management

Time management can help you accomplish your work more efficiently. One of the biggest mistakes in time management is thinking you have enough time. Plan your tasks ahead of time—when to work on them, how much time it will take you to accomplish them, and what tools or materials you might need or if you might need support. This will help you focus and deliver high-quality work on time or early.

Be flexible and adaptable. Even the best of plans may not work. There are some instances where we must re-prioritize some projects. For example, if Customer A has a big project due in two weeks, but suddenly Customer B has an important question that you need to answer quickly, you may have to pause the big project and answer the client's urgent question before going back to working on the big project for Customer A. This way, both clients will be happy with your stellar service, because Customer A will never know, and you will still finish the project on time.

Switching tasks and working under short deadlines can be nerve-racking, but do not let that stress you out too much. Write a plan and then *focus* on executing it. Letting go of distractions will help. Remember, you've got this!

Be a team player

Team players are those who "work well with others." Being a team player will help you succeed, and it will benefit your employer too. To work well with teams, show that you are reliable, responsible and ready to help. Actively listen to other people's points of view, show respect and support. Be a problem solver. You may have to tackle challenges and be flexible and not stubborn. Being a good team player also means being accountable and recognizing when you are wrong (if you indeed were wrong).

Finally, be kind, always. You never know who may become your next boss, or who may join you at the next job. The world is smaller than you think, and bad news spreads quickly.

Empathy

Being kind brings us to empathy, another important quality that will let you sparkle. Empathy means understanding and putting yourself in another person's place and trying to see what he or she might be feeling. This will help make a connection and improve relationships at and beyond work.

Sometimes, you might see your boss grumpy or upset for no apparent reason. Instead of being grumpy too (which is not a good idea), try being extra kind. It is not appropriate to ask about any personal details, but see if you can help with their work or give them space. It all depends on the character and the rapport you have with the person. Do not take every grumpiness personally. Perhaps your boss' child got sick, or perhaps they had a fight with their spouse. Empathy can help you connect with others in new ways.

Also, do not forget about being kind to and having empathy for yourself, my dear. In your free time, take a moment for self-care. For example, take a relaxing walk or a bath, watch a sunset or read a book you enjoy.

Accepting feedback & finding a mentor

Another great quality to consider is being curious, hungry for knowledge and open-minded. To grow, ask for feedback and please turn any of the pointers or seemingly negative remarks into opportunities for growth. This will give you direction about what to focus on and improve in your career.

Find a good mentor, if possible. It could be a teacher, a businessperson you admire, or a friend's mom. Select someone who is willing to offer advice. You can also learn a lot through the experiences of others by reading books. Dr. Seuss said, "The more that you read, the more things you will know. The more that you learn, the more places you'll go."

© 2019 Jola Burnett, "Leading with Soft Skills"

Chapter Six
Surviving Heartache

Beloved, do not worry before it happens, but heartache will revisit you and that is why we share it here. When the heart hurts because someone has rejected or disappointed you, it may seem like life is terrible and that nothing will improve. Some people call it having a broken heart, but your heart is never broken, Dear One. Your heart beats for the world, wanting to care for little children, older adults, people in pain, and even animals. Your heart wants to heal and strengthen the world.

Despite your heart's wonderful plans, when you are hurt, you may feel broken. You may get angry or cry, or you may not have the energy to do anything. You might wish to sleep all day. Everything seems more difficult when you have heartache. Some days, even the memory of an old pain can make you miserable all over again. Regrets about being an orphan, foundling, having lost a family member or friend, or experiencing rejection can resurface and you may feel sorry for yourself.

Coping well with heartache takes practice. First, accept your emotions. They are something that comes to your mind for a reason. You feel angry, sad, disappointed, frustrated, annoyed, irritated, alone, etc. Emotions are things people have. You have emotions. We have them. That is normal. When we have pain, we wish for it to go away—and quickly! We do not wish to be in anguish for one minute, if possible.

When we continue to hurt, then we look for ways to escape it. Since the pain continues, we must allow time to pass before it lessens and becomes more manageable. We feel better with time than we do the minute something makes us feel bad. We must allow time for us to heal.

At this point, it is useful to take the focus off your thoughts. If possible, do something that you enjoy, such as a watching a movie, reading a book, participating in sports or events, or something fun. Even better is completing acts of kindness and compassion toward others. Look for people who are also hurting and see if you can improve their condition by offering help or understanding. Pay attention to people who appear to have no one to speak to them. Smile at others. Make gifts for people. Assist others in completing activities that are difficult for them. Share food. Give a friend a hug.

Reaching out to others is one of the greatest ways to move beyond your pain and into loving the world. You are a precious gift to humanity. Everyone may not see it but that does not mean it is not true. Let me explain.

Imagine that a woman is at the hospital. Her son just had a seizure. The doctors are running tests and she cannot be in the same room, so she is standing outside. Her hands are shaking. She tells you that her son almost died in her arms. He had stopped breathing and she had been unable to open his jaws to help breathe into his mouth. Luckily, a friend visited and saved his life. You can tell when you see her that she is almost out of her mind with anguish. She has been crying. She looks at the door, waiting for a nurse to return and take her back to her son. In this moment of frantic desperation, you take some minutes and speak with the woman. Maybe you did not have the best day yourself. You are also at the hospital visiting someone. Instead of dwelling on your problem and feeling your pain, you speak to the woman and listen to her story.

After some time, you notice that the woman stops looking at the door. She is not pacing around anymore. Her voice is steady. Her eyes are more relaxed. She smiles a little now when she speaks. When the nurse comes for her, she smiles and thanks you. Suddenly, you feel better yourself. You were the one who made all the difference in the world for that woman then—and no one else.

I should know. I am that woman. This happened to my son and a stranger talked with me at the hospital. Instead of remembering the horror of that day at the hospital, I recall that a person I did not know before that day listened to my problems. What a wonderful person! It did not matter if they were rich or poor, young or old. They made me feel like I mattered, and they helped me get control of my emotions by talking to me. I returned to my son's side and focused on his needs and not mine. The circle was complete.

All the little things you do to be nice to others improves the world. You can let your pain make you a victim or you can use it as an opportunity to step out of your problems and assist others until your heartache becomes more manageable. We know that your situation may seem impossible, Dearest. We ask you to believe that with time and a lot of love, you will heal and maybe help others in the process. Hold on for us. One step at a time. One day at a time. One kindness at a time. You are needed. You matter. You will make a difference. We love you, Dear Heart. (((((HUG)))))

 # Anecdotes

Surviving Pain

Dear Hearts, let us now talk about surviving heartbreak. This something we all must face in life—whether young, old, sick, healthy, rich or poor. But do not fear. You are strong enough to get through to the other side of your pain. Acceptance can be key. Even though you may have lovely plans, some of these dreams could lead to heartache. Do you still dream despite the heartaches? Absolutely Yes.

Heartaches are part of life, my Sweethearts. The trick is to find the Good. Always look for the good, my Darlings. Look for the helpers. Amid sadness, loneliness and despair, that will be your strength, your rock! I like to say, "Keep your head up." This only means to hold your head high, no matter what troubles may challenge you. You are bigger than your fears, your trials, and your hurts.

Dear Ones, you must nurture yourselves. Simply put, Be Good to Yourself. This often has to do with putting away that broom that you may beat yourself up with for your mistakes. I've found we are often hard on ourselves when we are enveloped in sadness. We blame ourselves. But again, heartache is part of life, my Dears—not meant to be our downfall, but to teach us. All of life is here to teach us: to be gentle, loving, and giving, and to care for our lost and shipwrecked brothers and sisters.

My Sweethearts, this is easier said than done. However, when we rise from our pain to help another, we free ourselves from pain. We can fly above it and beyond it. Then we will know that the pain is only temporary, and that happiness waits around the next corner.

Life is like a roller coaster ride. There will be highs and lows; the trick is to hold on, breathe, enjoy the gifts of life, and be brave when you start down those hills. Dear Ones, your hearts will endure as will you. Your dreams will change throughout your lives. Your attitudes toward your dreams and your life will also change. Change is an inevitable part of life. This is something we can count on, so we must roll with these changes whether we see them as good or bad.

My Sweethearts, you can be the hero of your own story. Even more, you can be the hero in someone else's story. Your life can be a shining example to others as they too attempt to soothe their own pain. But even greater, you can see your life as a gift. No matter what, the gift of life is immeasurable, unlike any gift you could receive. Life is love; sharing, giving, and Being Love. Your life allows you to be what you choose. Dear Hearts, you have a wellspring of strength and love within you. To give this away means it will come back and be renewed. You mustn't think that your actions are inconsequential. The opposite is true. Every action you take has a ripple effect, like dropping a pebble into water. Every act of kindness—a smile, a hand held out, a hug, a word to console—these things are priceless.

Remember, my Sweethearts, be good to yourself as well.

This is your weapon against your heartaches. Being good to you means that if you're tired, you rest; if you need a hug, hug yourself if necessary; it means that you forgive yourself for your mistakes. It means that you tell yourself good things, such as: I am worthy; I am a good person; I deserve love; I can solve problems; I am a winner; I am talented; I am loving and giving. You must remember these affirmations, my loves. This is a truth of life: You Are Beautiful!

© 2019 Dr. Shanni Dover, "Surviving Pain"

Chapter Seven
Physical Pain

Physical pain is a challenge for us all, Darling. Some of us have little pain. Others of us endure regular pain and more of us go through periods of suffering due to illnesses or injuries. While we wish that you would never hurt, that is not the way that life is. We can complain, cry, and get angry, or we can cope, adapt, and find solutions to make life more tolerable.

Oh, do not worry if you cry. We all do sometimes when the frustration is too much or the level of discomfort that we experience is high. Some people may caution you against crying or request that you stop, but with us here and in your private time alone, you may cry as you need and then when you are finished, you can plan how to improve your situation.

Others may not understand what you experience or the level of aching or ill feelings you might have. People often cannot understand what you are going through if they have not experienced it or at least have known someone else who did. We expect them to know, but many times, they will not.

Medical professionals have tools and diagnostics that assist them in determining what is wrong with us and with experience, they have an awareness of our pain levels. However, you are unique and the way that your body feels things may differ from another person's experience.

We will give you some power. You are your best advocate.

An advocate educates others about your situation. If you are able, do not expect anyone else to explain for you. Politely and patiently state what you need or describe things so that others can comprehend your situation. If you are unable because you feel unwell or have had difficulty doing this, then select someone who may assist you in explaining.

Next, we hope that you have regular medical care. Even those of us who have good medical support encounter situations where we need to care for ourselves until we can get assistance. Others of us are beyond medical facilities at times or cannot afford to go to a doctor. You may do things on your own to improve some situations, but please assure us that if your situation does not get better, then you will consult a medical professional. While we fuss over your health in a motherly way, it is one of the ways this family loves you.

In fact, you can assist medical professionals in finding solutions to reduce your pain. Describe your symptoms well. As an advocate for your health, ask them to help you explore the causes for the pain and if something does not work, you can contact them and let them know you are not feeling better. Many people expect the first thing a doctor prescribes to work, but your body may not respond to the medicine in the predicted manner.

Medicine is one way to cope with pain and medical professionals may use a variety of methods to assist you. They may recommend physical therapy if you have been injured and over a series of visits with the therapist helping you move your body in ways that assist it in healing, you may feel a lot better. They could recommend equipment such as braces that stabilize a part of your body that is experiencing discomfort. Surgery may be required to alleviate the pain, but usually if that is the case, your suffering would be severe and you might be happy to get rid of it, surgery or not. They would also give you a shot to calm you before surgery too. Though I worried a lot about surgeries before I had them, when I received the shot, I felt in peace.

Be a student for your health and consistently seek advice from medical professionals. Ask for additional things that you can do to assist your healing. Doctors or nurses may suggest things to do at home to help you to feel more comfortable. Office visits can feel rushed, so plan what is most important for you to ask your doctor before you go.

At times, you may see others experience physical pain and not have the ability to do much to help. We must respect each person's right to determine what to do about their health if they are adults. If they are children in pain, then we should notify adults to determine what to do. Do not delay if a child is hurting and get help for them as quickly as possible.

If an adult is in pain, ask them if there is anything that they would like you to do or if there is a doctor or a person who they would like you to contact. It is not your fault that they have pain if you are unable to assist them. This is a part of life. Knowing that someone cares about them and is keeping them company makes a difference, though at times a person does not wish to have company and if they ask you to give them time alone, you should respect that. If a person seemed unwilling to have medical attention but they have lost consciousness in relation to their pain, then contact an adult or a medical professional.

Sometimes, we don't believe people who say they are in

pain or have discomfort. Others may have taught us to ignore or downplay people's pain. Trust that what a person says they need is true, until that is proven otherwise. In my experience, people tell the truth about their pain and even understate it more than they lie about it.

Learning about the causes behind pain and ways to cope with it makes us fear it less, so whenever things overwhelm you, switch into student mode and ask questions to learn more about what can be done to lessen any suffering for you or another person. Having health conversations may inspire people to produce a new solution or remind them of something they have tried before that worked in a similar situation. Do not expect doctors and nurses or other health professionals to tell you everything you ever needed to know. Ask if there is anything else that can help you feel better.

Distractions help me cope with discomfort when I am healing. If I have a muscle injury, reading helps get my mind off my injury. Other times, such as when I have a headache, watching a funny movie helps. A warm shower is a soothing distraction when I feel achy. When my pain was at its worst one time, counting helped me to meditate and relax my body so the pain was not as intense.

On rare occasions, someone will suggest something to do for pain that is harmful. Some websites may propose strategies that will do more harm than good. There is a considerable amount of unproven information on the Internet and trusting your health to that could be a risk. Consulting medical professionals is the first line of defense for your health. If that is not possible, then ask adults. If a young person shares an idea to try, then ask adults or medical professionals before attempting it.

When you are in doubt about what to do about your health, or when you do not have the money to visit medical professionals but are concerned, call or visit a nurse or doctor to learn if your situation requires medical care. I used to think that nurses would not talk to me on the phone if I was not coming into the office, but doctors have encouraged me to call and ask if I need to make an appointment or if I should be okay at home. If the situation is serious, they will tell you to come in immediately. In times of need, there are ways to care for your health. Without good health, you cannot do all the fabulous things you are meant to do with your abilities and make your dreams come true.

If you are in physical pain now, Dearest Heart, we are with you and wanting the best for you. Keep pursuing that path to feeling better. Do not give up on something so important. (((((HUGS)))))

Chapter Eight
Ability

Darling, people are like clouds. They have different shapes and sizes but the light shines through them all. If we only look at the shapes of the clouds, we do not see the most special part. What is most beautiful is how the sun shines through them and that is the same way with people. We have different abilities—strengths and weaknesses—and that makes us as unique from one another as clouds. One cloud is not better or worse than another. They all fill the sky and are part of nature. We are the same.

When you look at yourself, you may see someone who is much like everyone else, but different too. Or you may think that you are not similar. Inside you, the light still shines through. Like the sun, your spirit shines when you are compassionate and caring for others, and when you enjoy life and use your abilities and passions to add beauty to the world. You or others at times may focus on how we look, act, walk, talk, and experience life.

Some unfortunate people are disturbed when we are not the same as others. Bullies may act out against people and blame our differences. Society treats some people with preference and others do not receive that same treatment. People are not often shown the beauty of a world full of different clouds in the sky—each of us shining our own way.

You may do things differently. Your speech may be a challenge. You may listen, see, walk, or use your hands in ways that are less common. You may use a wheelchair, hearing aids, cochlear implants, hearing devices, a cane, glasses, or something to assist your walking. Your life may have accommodations that assist you in living, such as a service animal, ramps, or dots in your living area. Perhaps you attend counseling for trauma. Maybe you experience pain regularly. There are unlimited ways that people and their lives may be shaped, like the clouds.

If you look up at the clouds, the variety of shapes is magnificent. If they were all the same, then we would have nothing to admire. People who take pictures of clouds in sunrises, sunsets, and at other times appreciate what makes each one unique. The sun or the moon may shine around the edges or come through the clouds in rays or in bursts of light. Depending on the time, clouds may appear pink, purple, orange, gray, black, white, green, red, yellow, silver and other colors.

Because we are your family, we take a picture of you, put it on the wall and look at it and think about how much you mean to us and how fantastic it is that you are exactly the way you are. (Smile.)

We do not wish you to be someone else or to do things in another way that is not the best way for you. This does not mean that people will understand what assists you in a superior manner. They are not you and do not see through your eyes and the light does not shine through them in the same places that it comes through you.

Allow the sun to beam into your life in the way that it does.

Since others may not understand, then as your best advocate, patiently explain what would improve your life. For example, some people have a hard time walking. Some will choose a cane, walker, scooter, or wheelchair to help with mobility. They may have a vehicle adapted so that they may drive using a wheelchair. If they are in a wheelchair, they may need ramps, devices to help them grab things, a service animal, an attendant to help them dress or cook, or others forms of assistance. People who use mobility devices often attend college and become professionals and support themselves financially.

People who have difficulty hearing may choose hearing aids, an assistive listening device, sign language, a service animal to assist with nearby sounds, captioned words, or a cochlear implant. They may need interpreters or captioners when they attend events where they cannot hear. They may request information be written down, since hearing can be more difficult than reading for them. Some people with deafness who use sign language may understand things more easily through a sign language interpreter. People with hearing loss or deafness may attend a school for people with deafness, or they may attend college using captioned lectures or sign language interpreters. Many people with hearing loss or deafness live professional lives just like others.

If people do not see well or are blind, they may use magnification devices to make things appear larger, glasses, large print to read, a cane to walk, a service animal to guide them, Braille-raised print that they read with their hands, and things around the house to help them feel the settings on devices in their homes and label the colors of their clothes and the values of their money. Cell phones have applications that help them adapt to the world better, such as screen readers that read aloud the words on the screen, magnifiers, audio-guided maps, and money identifiers. Education about ways to do things without vision may give a person with vision loss or blindness greater independence. People with blindness may master public transportation, attend a school for people who are blind, or attend college where they receive written materials in Braille or using magnification. Blindness or vision loss is no indication that a person may not live and work independently.

If a person has cognitive or psychological differences, they may need counseling, a behavioral specialist, additional training, medicine, an attendant to help with life skills, specialized classes, or to learn methods to assist them with adapting to their environment. People with cognitive or psychological differences often find ways to assist them with their needs, attend college, and lead professional lives. While a person's I.Q. or mental health state used to exclude people from college, that is less true now and in the United States, for example, people with Down's Syndrome attend college, participate in government and leadership—and have fun!

People who are in regular pain may need physical therapy, pain management, medicines, regular medical care, and other coping strategies. Depending on how the pain affects their behavior, they may study or work from home. They can still achieve goals and dreams beyond what others can imagine.

With more technology available to assist people with their abilities, independent living is more common worldwide. With advocacy teaching others about how we can adapt to our home and workplaces, fewer people misunderstand abilities. More focus is now placed on what a person can do, instead of what she or he cannot do.

Diseases can affect any person at any time. Accidents can change the way we live in an instant. We can criticize the clouds for their differences or appreciate them. If we get angry at the clouds for the way they are, they do not change. Best to appreciate their uniqueness.

If someone gives you problems because of your differences, educate them about you. Some people use a sense of humor about their condition so that others will listen. If self-advocacy does not work with someone and they persist in being disrespectful or bullying, then share it with a professional who can offer support and guidance. If one person is not helpful, then ask another, or ask their superior. Ask them if they will be helpful for you or if they recommend someone else. Advocacy is not always simple.

Sometimes, it may take weeks, months, or years of advocacy for the situation to improve. Some must learn laws in their area that protect people. We are sorry if that is your situation, Dear Heart. Continue your advocacy so that you and others with similar circumstances will have a better future. Without education and advocacy, others will remain in a state of ignorance regarding your needs and lifestyle. Without awareness, they may make people's lives more difficult when they could simplify them.

Anecdotes

Lessons Learned from Dis-Ability

It's taken me a long time, but I've finally worked out that it's who I am and not what I do that is most important in life. Some people who seem to be so amazing with what they do end up being a disappointment when you encounter their lack of character. I experienced feelings of rejection from before I was born from my mother, and I never felt really wanted or loved by my family. As a result, I was always looking to please others and earn their love (especially that of authority figures). Also, as a long-time sufferer of Major Depressive Disorder and chronic fatigue, I've spent years doing and doing things and then crashing, and then repeating the pattern. Each time, though, the recovery time has become longer and longer. During these down times, I have learned my biggest lessons:

1. Even if I do nothing, I am still valuable

My identity was so wrapped up in my performance that I wasn't sure I would be enough without proving my worth. My down times forced me to look at myself and my behaviours and to do the work on my character that was sorely needed. This work is a luxury that busy people rarely have, since it requires a lot of aloneness, quietness and self-reflection. I've now come to love *who I am*, rather than *feeling loved* because of *what I did*.

2. Character is developed out of the spotlight

I wanted to rise to the top like a skyscraper so everyone could see me and tell me how wonderful I was, but that type of fame is not lasting and doesn't bring true self-worth. If you want a tall building to last, you must dig down deep into the earth and build strong foundations. Creating character is an unseen work that goes on under the surface but is foundational to any lasting work that others see.

3. True and lasting impact comes through relationships

There is a quote that I love that applies here. Bill Wilson said, "To the world you may be one person; but to one person you may be the world." What relationships are you neglecting by being everything to everyone else? It never felt important enough to me to be just a wife or a mother. I had to be out there getting everyone to love me! It's always harder to walk in close relationships with everyday people in your life because that challenges you to change. Who is your one person? Be the friend that she or he needs. YOU are the gift in their lives, far more than your acts of service toward them. Take time to build relationships and be content that you are having a true and lasting impact—in one life at least.

© 2019 Jill Magnussen, "Lessons Learned from Dis-Ability"

Be the Most Amazing You!

What is ability all about? Many of us have areas in which we excel and feel comfortable in and others that challenge us. It's not always easy to live in a fast-changing world with so much to tackle and to understand. Sometimes, we're overwhelmed, especially if we perform differently, behave differently or have what others may call deficits or disabilities that hinder us in countless ways.

There are many stories of famous people who had and have challenges of various kinds—some they could overcome, some they had to adapt to and some whose challenge became their greatest strength. What's so important in all these stories and individuals, and to us, is that no matter the difficulty, they never gave up. They continued to find ways and answers to help themselves learn, grow and thrive.

Do you have a disability or medical condition? You're not alone and it's nothing to be ashamed of or to hide. People with disabilities include actors, actresses, celebrities, singers, world leaders, scientists, inventors and many other famous people. There are also millions of people in the world who aren't famous or well-known who live with, battle and overcome their disabilities every day.

Leonardo da Vinci (1452–1519) was a man of many talents. He was an artist, inventor, scientist, engineer and a writer. Yet he had learning and thinking differences such as writing backward and strange spelling that set him apart from others. These are now considered character traits of a person with dyslexia. Despite these differences, his achievements are still celebrated today.

Thomas Edison (1847–1931) was thought of as a difficult and hyperactive student. He came up with effective ways to learn and study on his own that helped him both make and shape history. He invented the phonograph, the motion picture camera, and the light bulb. Walt Disney had learning challenges but became an animator, cartoonist and the creator of Disneyland.

Whoopi Goldberg, who is an actress and comedian, doesn't let her learning difficulties interfere with her goals and her successful career. Jess Thom, a public speaker and advocate for the rights of people with disabilities, was diagnosed with the neurological condition, Tourette syndrome, in her twenties, and she uses a wheelchair today. Tourette's is a constant source of her creativity.

When I was a child and first began to write, mirror writing showed up. The only way anyone could read what I wrote was to hold it up to a mirror. Only then, the reversed words and letters magically corrected themselves. I had to cope with and understand what being atypical was. I taught myself how to learn things differently because I discovered that conventional methods of teaching and learning didn't always work for me. Even when I was in graduate school earning a master's and doctorate, I had to accept the fact that the way I learned was different. I also had to not judge myself harshly or see myself as less than anyone else because of this. It may have taken me longer to learn and understand but that didn't stop me from receiving my degrees, nor should anything stop you.

No matter the differences and unique abilities/disabilities that you have, don't let anything stand in the way of following your heart, your dreams and what excites you. Whether challenges, setbacks or temporary defeat are present, remind yourself that they don't define you. Focus instead on your abilities, talents and strengths and develop them as best as you can. Decide that you can overcome whatever is in your path to be and become the most amazing You!

© 2019 Dr. Jo Anne White, "Be the Most Amazing You!"

Dr. Jo Anne White is an international #1 bestselling and award-winning author and speaker and is recognized as a Goodwill Global Ambassador for her civil and humanitarian work in education, entrepreneurship, coaching and women's issues. As a certified life, spiritual and business coach, and energy master teacher, she empowers and inspires men and women, their families and businesses to achieve greater health, wellness and success and to thrive and triumph. Dr. White is also the founder of the Power Your Life Network and Executive Host and Producer of the Power Your Life Shows. She's been featured online and in publications such as Good Housekeeping, More, and WebMD and has appeared on radio and television networks as NBC, CBS, FOX and Voice America and at www.drjoannewhite.com

Chapter Nine
Motherly Advice about
Doing the Right Thing

When we do what is good and appropriate, and what benefits the most people, then our lives are easier. Most people gravitate toward goodness in others. When we do what is wrong and commit acts that violate laws or rules that are designed to protect others, then the penalties and consequences make life uncomfortable. Most people fear or keep their distance from people who break laws and rules, or from those who do not show concern for the safety or benefit of others.

This does not mean, Darling, that you were born knowing what is best for most people. Others may have shown you how to do things that have gotten you into trouble. You may have found trouble without any help. Systems are created to protect people in countries all over the world because people accidentally or on purpose hurt others and societies wish to protect people.

Some of you live in areas where war may be common and that is more difficult to understand how some societies will harm others. We do not take political sides here because we are a family inspiring you to be the best that you can. Our goal is not to convince you that one political system is better than another. We are humanitarians and peacemakers with you and the world, Dearest One. Our desire is that when you become your best, your decisions and beliefs will improve the world. You will reach your own conclusions about how you will help that come to be.

People may be arrested or tried in court for harming or killing others or for committing crimes such as stealing, damaging others' property, drinking or doing drugs and then driving, speeding while driving, selling drugs that may make others ill or die, or not respecting other people's bodies and hurting or violating them. These crimes are penalized by law and justice systems.

There are other ways to do the wrong thing. If you lie about another person, not telling the truth may cause that person several problems. Doing that to other people is not the right thing to do. It is not always easy, but doing the right thing has fewer negative consequences. Someone who lies about others may lose friends or get in trouble. The person that they lied about may take revenge that could result in violence.

If two people are in a relationship and one of them wants to date you, then you may hurt all three of you. Many societies punish or frown upon this behavior. If one person in a relationship with another person says they wish to be with you, then they need to be free from connections to another person. If not, then the other person may harm you or them. People have been killed for getting involved with a partner who is committed to someone else by marriage or otherwise. If you fight back, then you might harm them. Their breaking up with someone else to be with you can also hurt the couple whose relationship you are helping destroy.

Seek relationships with uncommitted people where you

can be with one person without harming another and your relationships will feel more blessed and less cursed. Your respect for others' relationships and commitments demonstrates to your current or future loved one that you will take your relationship with him or her seriously.

Love lets us find the best in ourselves. When used properly, love is a powerful force that improves the world. When you derive your strength from doing the right thing and caring for others and the world, then you will find rewards and benefits from life that you cannot find any other way. People will think well of you. Strangers or others may commit acts of kindness in your favor for no reason. Dearest Heart, we believe that when you give, you also receive in return. While at the beginning, that may motivate you, as you grow into your best self, doing the right thing feels so good that you share love with the world just for the joy of it.

The more you make the most beneficial choices for all, the fewer your problems will be and the greater your blessings and feelings about yourself. If you are a nice, generous, helpful, and respectful person, then you will appreciate yourself more than people who are mean, greedy, problematic, and disrespectful. You will make mistakes. We all do, Darling. Do not let that discourage you from perpetuating goodness in the world. Forgive yourself because of the kindness you will share with others again.

Give in ways that do not harm you. Sometimes, others will ask you to do things that do not benefit you or make you feel uncomfortable. Do not do these things because you think love is always doing what is asked of you. You and all of us have the right to say no when we feel something is wrong for us, and to be listened to and understood.

If someone asks or demands that you do things in the name of love that you believe will harm you or your loved ones, do not associate with that person if possible and seek help from a professional authority. Ask a safe professional, teacher, professor, police officer, or member of your place of worship to advise you about what action to take. It is okay to seek the advice of several professionals to get a rounded opinion or to answer more of your questions.

For many of us, our faith in God and our houses of worship helps keep us focused on maintaining a strong character with better behavior. Your faith is a personal decision, but we felt it important to share that many of us use prayer and our faith communities to complement our lives. We do not share the same religions and we are a family who worships God in different ways. Those of us who agree on this believe that it is an important aspect of our lives. This does not mean that any house of worship will feel like the right family for you. You will determine if it makes you feel accepted and directs you to become a better person and give to the world using your special talents.

Regardless of your faith, benefiting humanity is the goal and not harming or reducing it. We take care of others, assist them, share necessities or gifts, listen, value their abilities, and encourage them. We respect that they own things they do not want damaged, have pets that they love, and own land or other things that do not belong to us. They own their own person and belong to people who love them, such as their family. We do not have the right to force them to like us or be with us and they are protected from us if we try to make them act against their desire. If they say no to us, they mean it and we should respect that. We do these things because we do not want anyone to harm us or our loved ones, make us do things we do not want to do, or damage or take our property.

Many of us believe that what goes around, comes around, and so if we perform harmful acts, then harm will come to us; but, if we love the world, then that will return to us. This cycle is not instant, but it can be. Often, if we hurt another person, then hours, days, months, or years later we discover that a similar harm came to us later. By living it, "what comes around, goes around" has been proven true to us. Do not treat others as you do not wish to be treated; love others as you wish to be loved, with respect for their wishes and their shining hearts.

You may not see the good in everyone all the time and indeed, some people may be dangerous. Avoid the scary ones as often as possible and keep company with people who uplift you, value your talents, and encourage you to do the right thing. As you become stronger, this will enable you to one day reach out to others in serious need, such as people who are orphans and foundlings, or are homeless, have different abilities, or are in pain or sick.

Anecdotes

Give Yourself All the Love You Need

Dear Child, I hope you are feeling loved today, because you are important and loved just the way you are. Believe in yourself and everything is possible. Sometimes, we face hard things and feel that people are mean to us or that they do not understand our situation. But remember, you are not alone.

Your life has a special meaning and it is important that you find your calling. You were born for a reason and you need to find out what it is. Only you know the answer to that question, and you must listen carefully to what your heart whispers.

Strength comes from overcoming. Whatever you are going through in life will make you strong. One day you will look back and say: "I did it." Look at the bright side of life and stick to everything kind and caring. Find the right direction in life by listening to your inner voice—and finding out what your heart pumps for.

Every person has something to give this world. The love we need is within us, and we need to give the love to ourselves and spread it to others. We can become the energy of Love, but we must also forgive those who have done us wrong so that our heart can heal.

Whatever the circumstances are, make the best of it and stay positive. Take good care of yourself and your body; find your inner Mother and Father to take care of you in every possible way and every day. Find out what is best for you and stay away from everything that is not good for you.

Drop everything that makes you feel bad and hang on to things that make you happy. Distance yourself from negative people and things. What's the most important thing in life? It's love. And love begins with you.

Work hard for things that are important to you and stay focused—even if others don't understand you or why it is so important to you. Not everyone will understand you. That's okay. Be yourself anyway. You need to make choices that feel right for you, and not pleasing others.

Everything happens for a reason. Sometimes it's very hard to understand why something happens. Just trust God and His will. Things happen because life wants to teach us something and we need to grow and learn. Difficult lessons often help us find a new direction and find ourselves.

Life is a mystery and we are here to grow and live it to the fullest: to love, to be happy and to do good things for one another. Do what you love, and your purpose will soon follow. You were gifted with something that you need in life; to give this world something of you and to leave it a little bit better place than it was when you found it.

Use your gifts and do everything you can to build your future around what you love. But don't let anyone take advantage of you. Some people want to use others for personal purposes. Don't let that happen.

Find balance in your life and relationships; determine who belongs in your life and who doesn't. So always follow your heart, it knows the truth and is your best guide and compass. Also know that bad behavior is the result of a lack of love. If someone treats you badly, that person's lack of love is spilling over on you—it has nothing to do with you. Stay kind to yourself and others always but also set boundaries for how you let people treat you. You can show compassion and distance yourself from negative feelings.

Life isn't always easy, but hardships are often blessings in disguise. Later, you will understand why it all happened, as life gives you more experience and wisdom. You must also forgive yourself for letting people in your life break your heart. Only by forgiveness can a broken heart be mended.

Be honest with yourself and others. You can't "save" another person; everyone has to save himself. You can help others and give them tools to work out their problems, but they must handle their own.

Focus on your own life and wellbeing. Find balance and happiness in your life—through love and forgiveness—and you will soon show others the right way in life with your own example. Find your "why" and the rest will follow.

Stand before a mirror and tell yourself that you are beautiful and worthy of love, and others will see you the way you see yourself. Whatever happened in the past, let it strengthen you. You are stronger than you think, and you have the power to change.

When you change your life, you change the world, because love changes the world. Love begins with you, and you are Love. Do good things to others and good things will come back to you in many unexpected ways because life is an echo. What you send out comes back.

Accept people as they are because it is impossible to change anyone. Love changes people. Love yourself, because love heals everything, and all wounds, including a broken heart. Love is the most powerful force on Earth. Anything you do, do it with love.

We need to build a world with love, kindness, empathy and compassion because that's the only way for humanity to survive. Everything is possible when we vibrate the energy of Love.

With Love,

Jaana Uolamo

~ *Mother*

© 2019 Jaana Uolamo, "Give Yourself All the Love You Need"

How to Love the World When You Feel Angry

Loving the world when you feel happy
is easy;
loving the world when you feel angry
is not.

There is a trick, though—
in your mind, roar like a lion until your face turns red;
stomp your feet as if a beast has escaped the zoo.
Scream: *Anger, you will not win.*

Then watch Anger run away
like a coward
because Anger is a first cousin to Fear.
Anger is AFRAID.

And once Anger leaves,
you are free
to love the world
and be.

© 2019 Michele Kelly, "How to Love the World When You Feel Angry"

Bloom Your Own Life

Dear Child,

When you face times where your heart is challenged by doing what's right for yourself, do not be afraid that you cannot make the right decision.

Life's challenges are normal and are never meant to intimidate you, but they are rather a part of life's process for you to learn about life and its beauty, for you to be able to grow up into a beautiful person.

As your mother, my love is always there, even though I may not be with you physically now.

You are forever dear to me, forever in my heart, and that's important for you to know.

My advice is given out of my deep love and care for your well-being, and my wishes are that you will not falter in life because you are alone without my physical presence.

Hence, my Beloved Child, should you at any time find yourself yearning for Mum's advice, recall these few things that I am listing for you here:

When You Face Life's Tests

There will always be testing times in your life, tests that seem to bring you pains and fear, that seem to mean nothing but sorrow and suffering. During such times, be courageous to handle your tests with the best of you. Know that you can pass each one, that you are capable enough, and know that there is always hope even though at times you may not feel so.

I will still be watching over you, and for as long as you keep my advice in your heart and draw strength from it, you will succeed.

When You Feel Lonely

There will be times that you will feel so lonely in your heart that you may wonder if you are able to be happy. Loneliness, my Dearest Child, is experienced even by those who live with many people surrounding them. It is a heavy feeling of wishing to have people to love you, be with you, and even keep you company for the sake of feeling less unhappy.

Have no fear to embrace loneliness and use such times by finding something you think you would like to do that can give those who are unhappy some joy and cheer. There are many people out there who feel as lonely or as unhappy as you may experience, and by doing something that brings joy and cheer for others to uplift their spirit, you can feel your own spirit being uplifted. Don't be afraid to give; don't be afraid to share your life with people who may need your supporting love.

Follow Your Conscience

Whenever you are advised by those around you to participate in activities of life, do be steady and clear-minded that every activity you perform must never hurt yourself or another person. The world is made up of all kinds of personalities, and you need to be aware that not everything you do is suitable for you. My advice is simple, my Beloved Child—with any act you perform, follow your good heart and your conscience. That way, you will find more peace and live with less guilt, which will eventually help you feel at ease and at peace with all!

Don't Despair, Bloom Your Own Life

Whenever you feel that others are happier than you and that your life is in shambles, do not despair. Life has its beauty for all. Be courageous to follow your heart's talents and strengths and live as best as you can using those talents to live well. When you feel deeply with your heart and do whatever you need to do with love and passions, you can bloom your own capabilities and success!

My Darling Child, this advice is from my heart to yours.

Keep it with you and draw strength from it. You are more than what you think you are!

    With love, Mum

Chapter Ten
Your Dreams Matter

One of the most important things your family can do is encourage you to follow your dreams. What are your dreams? Maybe you have not thought about this before. What do you enjoying doing? What do you do well? If you could have three wishes granted, what would they be? While some wait for wishes to be granted, most of us work to make our dreams a reality. I wanted to be an author one day and now I am, though my journey took years. Dreams do not often come true instantly but are the result of continuous effort that we sustain until our dream is realized.

Some of our dreams are the result of things we have seen that we know must be improved. For example, you may wish that there were fewer orphans and foundlings in the world and more happy families. Your concern could also be that orphans and foundlings have more community support and resources —or even more fun! Or, you may have seen people have difficulty with their abilities and think it should be easier for them to get what they need to adapt. Perhaps you have witnessed violence and want to work toward greater world peace.

Bad things inspire good dreams as much as good things do.

Writing, drawing, or recording your notes can be a great resource for examining your dreams so you can revisit them later and add to them. For example, if you want to make a video game, you may start by writing a storyline and then drawing sketches of characters for the game. Then you would plan to make the game and locate people to help you make it happen. You may have to research and interview gamers to prepare to meet your goal. List steps you need to take and then make a calendar for when you will accomplish each goal. Yes, Darling, we are certain that you can create a reality that is better than a dream.

Many orphans and foundlings realize that the world has problems that need fixing and they have seen ways they would like to help, such as in building communities to support youth without parents. To make such a dream come true, you may organize the details and research and locate resources over a period of years. One person might wish to build an orphanage, while a person who has skills selling things may want to raise money to construct one. A person who leads people well may assemble a team of people to use their abilities to complete their mission. Some dreams take years to see come true and when they do, Dearest One, you can believe it was worth the wait.

Part of having a successful plan is realizing that life will throw you curve balls. In baseball, a curve ball is pitched so that when the player hits it with a bat, it goes in an unexpected direction. Baseball players can often hit balls where they want them to land in the field, but a curve ball may make that impossible. They may hit the curve ball and it may spin behind them. When you have a curve ball in life, an unexpected problem, then do not walk away from the game and quit. Imagine if baseball was like that. The game would be over in minutes. Instead, when you go to bat, see that you have several opportunities to hit a ball.

Sometimes, things do not go as planned. It is possible in baseball to not hit the ball but when the pitcher hits your body with it, then you may walk to first base because the pitcher is not supposed to pitch it at you. You may not have a home run and score points yet, but you have made progress. Life is like baseball because you do not always have the power to choose how things will happen. However, you have a choice to remain at bat and to continue playing, as well as practicing and improving your game.

When I was learning softball, the cousin of baseball, I went to batting cages and parks to improve my ability to hit the ball. While many players on our team did not practice more often than at our team practices, my coach said she saw a difference when we practiced more often.

We used to get a gold metal star to place on our softball hats when we scored a home run. We all wanted the coveted four-star grand slam—and four gold stars for our softball cap! This is when a batter hits a home run when their teammates are on first, second, and third bases. When the batter of a grand slam runs into home plate, they have scored four points for their team by enabling three teammates to run home as well as running home for her or himself. After practice, I had developed a good eye and could hit a fast softball far. A pitcher pitched a fast ball to me, hoping to strike me out, but it was my preferred type of pitch! I hit it hard and it soared across the field, scoring a grand slam for our team. That would have been impossible if I had not practiced for hours and hours.

Family encouraged me and we do the same for you. If you

are striking out, keep going to the batting cages. Learn how to improve your abilities and coping skills.

We do not promise that life will be easy or that you will not have challenges. Overcoming your challenges makes life more special. If I had hit a grand slam the first time that I played softball, then I would not share the story with you now. That would have required no effort, so it would not have been a story. Because I worked hard for it, I learned that other people can do the same. Few of us are natural-born batters. When you see a batter at bat, you see his or her whole life of batting practices.

You can be terrible at anything and improve with dedication and the right teachers. If you are practicing and have dedication, but are not progressing, seek a teacher or a new instructor who presents information in a way that you learn best. Not everyone will instruct you the way that you learn solidly. Not everyone is a born teacher, either. Select your teachers and mentors, people who do things well and will guide you on your path.

If you wish to become an accountant, then you would not ask a lawyer how to do that. You would ask an accountant if you could volunteer with her or him to see an accountant's experience. If you enjoy it, then you would ask him or her about what education is needed and how to finance it. If you are taking classes already, then you could ask for advice when you do not understand how something works in the accounting world.

If you wish to become a lawyer, seek out a lawyer or two to learn from them. Aspiring artists seek mentor artists who use their preferred art materials and techniques. Future teachers may select mentors who teach the grade level and subject they wish to instruct. Those entering the medical field locate mentors who have similar interests in a branch of medicine. If you wish to play an instrument better, then you want an instructor who uses a method that benefits your style and preferences. For sports, you want mentors who display abilities and techniques that you wish to develop.

Not every professional is a good mentor, but when you find one that is knowledgeable and willing to make time for you, that is a good match. Do not give up on your mentor search if you feel that you need one. Like many of us, you have quite a list of mentors over a lifetime. You can only learn so much from school or college and then you need experience and connections to develop as a professional or entrepreneur starting your own business.

If you have different abilities and need to make adaptations because you use a wheel chair, have blindness or vision loss, hearing loss or deafness, or some other unique situation, locate someone who is a professional with similar abilities, though they may work in a different career from your chosen path. Professionals have many challenges and so someone facing the same ones you have will offer advice, technology resources, and useful connections to help you adapt to the work world.

Some of our mentors include famous people who we read about but have never met. People learn great amounts of information from books and many successful businesspeople read regularly to develop their skills and score their grand slams. We are cheering for you out in the stands. Go you! Go you! You can do it!

Anecdotes

Dreams

"Sometimes all we have is hope. Hold onto it with both hands and don't give up."
Amanda Ray @amandaray02

There is no magic formula and no one person knows the best way to achieve goals and dreams, for everyone has different life experiences.

Try different approaches, search the Internet, read personal growth books or find a mentor to guide you; it doesn't matter as long as you find the best method for you. Your dreams, your life, your choice.

It took me twenty years to fulfil my dream of travelling around Australia. The plan was to pack my car with my worldly possessions and drive around the country, stopping in towns or cities I liked, getting a job and staying for a while before moving on.

During those twenty years, I had numerous challenges to overcome: life-threatening illness, domestic violence, financial loss and job redundancies. There were times that I wanted to give up since everything seemed too hard. But what kept me going was my dream to travel around Australia. It gave me hope to keep going even when things seemed hopeless.

Now, I'm living my dream. It's not the whole of Australia, only Queensland, but it's a big state, taking two-three days' driving to get from one end to the other! It's not without its own challenges, but the experience, the people I am meeting, and the scenery is worth all of it.

The feeling of knowing that you did it on your own is the feeling of success. And, that's why dreams are important.

"Remain calm and focused on your end goal when life doesn't work out as you hoped."
Amanda Ray @amandaray02

© 2020 Amanda Ray, "Dreams"

The Kite of Freedom, a short story

"I will find a way to set birds free," the boy said. "After you pet a cat or a dog, they are free to walk and run around, but when you pet a bird, they are unable to fly in the sky, and that's where they belong."

"Why are you so curious about the birds?" the old man asked. "If you don't trap those birds, your master will fire you because he pays you to cage them."

The boy said, "When my parents died in a car accident, all of their things were snatched by my relatives. The things which I inherited were not mine. I am not worried about the things, but about the love and joy I had. My parents helped me with shelter and food, but also gave me love, happiness, care, joy, and freedom. Freedom to play, learn, explore and dream. My new dream is to set birds free."

"How would you do that?" the man asked.

"I don't know how, but I am pretty sure that I will find a way," the boy said.

* * *

While roaming around the forest, lost in thoughts about finding a way to keep his words, the boy found a black and white feather. He picked it up and thought, "You will find a way!"

The boy quit working for the bird vendors and decided to free all the birds in a few days. He shared this idea with his old friend.

His friend asked, "Don't you think it is a crime? Entering businesses without their permission and setting birds free?"

"Should we call this act a crime only when you do this to a human?" the boy asked.

"No! Fundamental rules are equal for all creatures," the man said.

The boy asked, "Why don't people care about animals' feelings—even when they love them? Why do they imprison them with love?"

"Well, boy, this is not the only perspective," the man said. "The birds being tamed by humans are provided proper food and a hygienic environment. They don't die of hunger, cold, heat or disease because they are given vaccines. This makes their lives easier and safer. Look beneath the things, boy!"

After thinking, the boy said, "Maybe you are right. I was

wrong. I didn't look for this perspective. I lost my parents and was dropped in an orphanage, where I missed my parents' love a lot. After that, I worked as a slave for a group who trapped and sold birds, but I left them because I never wanted anyone or anything to go through the same pain. Sigh! Enough of this dream! I must look for a new job so that I can eat."

The man said, "When I said that there is another perspective, that doesn't mean that your perception is wrong. I am in my late seventies and I have seen that we all leave this planet, which results in either making others into orphans or becoming an orphan yourself. You know, the point to ponder is how can a boy who is so curious about the feelings of birds and other animals ignore the emotions behind his own dreams?"

"Wait, what? Did you just say the emotions of my dreams? How can dreams have emotions, when you can't even see their physical existence?"

His friend nodded. "Only when you believe in them with all your heart. A dream is created in your imagination, developed in your thoughts, designed in your ideas, reframed in your mind, listened to in your head, felt in your heart and touched in your soul. After being the creator of your dreams, how can you make them orphans? Your dreams can never be seen by others unless or until you make them true."

"I never want to leave my dreams," the boy said, "but what if they don't come true? What if I fail? What would I gain then?"

"Your thinking process stops you from pursuing your dreams by asking what happens if they don't come true," the man said.

"But what about the perspective you shared before?" asked the boy.

"Well, I belong to the old generation. I am the past and present, and you belong to the new generation. The present and future belong to you. We share a gap of time. The new generation will have new problems, new thoughts and for sure new solutions. We play our roles and fulfil our duties, and the best way to find your purpose is to listen to the beat of your heart and the call of your undeniable dreams."

The boy said, "I don't know how, but I will positively find a way because I will never let my dreams become orphans." Then, he ran away.

* * *

The boy roamed in the woods, thinking of how to help his dreams. He found another feather, but this time, it was a yellow feather. Two days passed. He found a squirrel whose leg was stuck under a log, rushed toward it, and removed its leg out from under the log. He rubbed its leg gently and then left the squirrel on a walnut tree so that it could find other squirrels as well as eat easily.

After two more days, the boy found a cat stuck in some tree branches. He helped free the cat, but as he rescued the cat, he accidently put his foot on a snake and the snake chased him. He ran and the snake almost bit him. The boy was shivering and moving back step by step, when suddenly an eagle appeared and took the snake away. The boy sighed and walked away. As he left, he found a black feather.

Lying in a garden and wondering about a solution for his

problems, the boy asked himself why after searching for solutions, he ended up hopeless. He took all the feathers out and looked at them, then at the sky for some moments. He closed his eyes.

Something fell on him and when he opened his eyes, he found it was a kite. A kid with his mom came to him to get his kite back, but the kid cried because the kite was torn. The boy was upset to see that child crying for his kite.

After the kid and his mother left, the boy started looking at the sky and then got up and shouted, "YES! I have found a way to my dream!" When he ran to the woods, he found a grey feather.

He created a kite made with colorful birds' feathers and decorated it with lights, so that people could enjoy kiting during the night too. He was almost done with his creation, but needed one more feather, so he went to the forest and searched for another feather and found a blue one.

The boy asked his friend to come along with him to the garden because he had to show him something. He asked his friend to wait for him at a point.

It was about sunset. Children were there with their families. A child shouted, "Look! What an amazing kite!" The people watched the boy's kite while the sun set. Almost everyone had turned their faces around to head to their homes when a girl shouted, "Wow! That's so amazing! The kite has lights too." Everyone was flabbergasted by the feathered kite that was decorated with lights and had made the night significant. Now, people searched for the owner of this new kite.

Then, the boy came forward and said, "My name is Eric. I

am an orphan. This kite belongs to me and I have created it. I would never have created it if I never had a dream to set birds free. It seemed hopeless to make my dream come true. Fortunately, an old pal persuaded me to believe in my dreams." He motioned for his friend to walk to him. "I was frightened that I might fail. Believe me, a dream is not about reaching your destination only, but is a process of making you grow and changing positively while pursuing your dreams.

His friend had walked from his viewing spot and his eyes lit up at the site of the miraculous kite. Eric smiled and said, "The day I intended to work for my dream, I found a black and white feather, which was a symbol that a positive change was coming. One day, I found a yellow feather and later rescued a squirrel. That feather was a symbol that the light is here with me to show me the right path."

"Another day," Eric said, "I rescued a cat and I myself was saved by an eagle who protected me from a snake's bite. After that, I found a black feather, which explained to me that an angel is here protecting me, my energy and my growth during my spiritual awakening. When I had the idea of making a feather kite, I found a grey feather, which symbolized that life had been hectic, and peace was arriving soon."

"When my kite was a feather away from being completed," Eric said, "I found a blue feather, which was a sign that my psychic abilities were unfolding. I would not have observed such deep things if I had never accepted, agreed and dared to make my dream come true."

"When I gave up on my dream," Eric said, "my friend told me that a dream is created in your imagination, developed in your thoughts, designed in your ideas, reframed in your mind, heard in your head, felt in your heart and touched by your soul, which means that dreams exist too." His cherished friend grinned because Eric had remembered his words.

Eric said, "I started this dream with a simple question: what is the purpose of wings if birds can't fly? What kind of love do you have for birds, if it is not letting them fly? I learned that the most important thing was to believe in myself. Only one thing helps you make your dreams come true; the act of investing in yourself is a way to discover the resources blessing you."

No one had met Eric before and they were in awe of his kite, so the people listened and watched his kite glow in the evening sky. "To free others, free yourself first. To make others believe in themselves and in their dreams, believe in yourself and in your dreams first. You have everything within yourself already but need to believe a bit more."

"A single wish of setting birds free has aided me to observe things intensely. Not only do those who are in cages or are imprisoned need your help, but you can surely make this world a better place by helping those who are already free," Eric said. "Happiness is not only about setting others free but is also about aiding them in achieving their true potential."

Eric's friend patted his back and smiled. This was his young friend's awakening. Eric said, "This dream helped me to make a kite that can be seen at night so that people can enjoy kiting during evenings, a solution for kite lovers that will help them enjoy it during summer holidays and keep them safe from the hot sun of day. Your dreams do not matter for you only but aid others as well."

Eric nodded at his friend. "Dreams are a blessed resource.

Whenever you feel like quitting your dreams, remember that you created them in your imagination, and you cannot leave them alone. Your dreams matter. I have named this kite, 'The Kite of Freedom' because it gave me a powerful message and lesson: WINGS ARE USELESS IF A BIRD CAN'T FLY."

As the people's faces were lit by the glow of The Kite of Freedom that Eric passed around for them to fly, they were certain of two things. Eric had flown and he would find a way to free the birds one day.

© 2019 Noorio Zehra, "The Kite of Freedom"

Chapter Eleven
Balancing Work and Family

The motherly life consists of completing daily work and devoting time to the care and needs of family. We are spending quality time with you, our family, right now. We want our darling child to succeed and make great contributions to the betterment of the world. We spend time with you so that you feel wanted and encouraged to develop your skills and be your best self.

Loved ones around you may be like family or perhaps your situation is unique where you have limited time with family or anyone like that. The devotion to family or our community is vital. We stopped our world to work on this gift of love for you because you matter so much to us.

One of the motherly gifts is to balance work and family and often mothers have different goals from fathers, but this does not have to be so. Many mothers put primary importance on their families, while fathers may place more value on being a good worker and providing for the family's needs. Whether our loved ones are the family we are born with or the one we choose for ourselves, without enhancing others' lives, the benefits of work pale. People matter. Without people, there is no work. Caring for people makes the world continue its good work.

Achieving balance is difficult between completing the work you have while caring for the people you love. Chores, jobs, and responsibilities must be met. Money needs to be earned and saved. People get sick or have bad days and need our emotional support. They may also require our assistance in completing their own tasks, such as homework. Which things are the most important? You only have so many hours in a day!

This is just it. You only have so many hours in a day and you do not know how many days you will have with each person. Live each day with grace, kindness, and love—as if you may not have another opportunity. We cannot guarantee that your loved ones will be here tomorrow. So, we treasure our loved ones each day.

Your heart is so giant inside that you cannot imagine its immensity. Your heart was designed to love the whole world. If you exercise it, you can love and care for thousands of people and work to assist them. We do love a few people right next to us in our lives and sometimes it feels like they are our entire world. We may be their world and they might not even tell us! They may think they have forever to tell you how they feel, or they may not be comfortable expressing their feelings.

We will lose people though, and we must be strong and continue caring about people everywhere we go. Though it may feel like we are here for one person, we are here for humanity. In books and on social media, we use GoldenHearts because we believe in loving the world. We have learned that many people need us and not just one. Like the mother who has three children or ten, we know that it is possible to spread the love to as many people as need it. How do we balance loving the world and work?

The easiest way to do it is to have work that complements your family life. Work where you have the time and ability left over to continue your dream work and spending quality time with the ones you love. Some mothers work at home to raise their families, but each person's choices are personal. Do what is best for you and those you love.

When you are needed away from work, you must consider this carefully. If you have a sick loved one and they need your care, do not immediately say that going to work is more important. If you can do so and if they are seriously ill, then you could request a personal day off from work. If you cannot, then search for solutions to ensure that people who need you are not left alone. Neighbors or friends may assist you. You may swap favors with friends or neighbors so that you help one another on a rotating basis. If you are able, you could pay someone to be there when needed. At the very least, arrange to have someone check in on your loved one and ensure that they are okay when you cannot be there.

We must be resourceful to balance work and family and be creative with our resources and time. Organizing time will benefit you. If you cook dinner for everyone, but work as well, then use free time to cook meals ahead of time so that the meals only need to be heated later. Or you could prepare cut vegetables ahead of time and keep it in containers for future use. Planning out your days and the use of the hours you have will help you accomplish twice as much. If you and a few loved ones have several appointments during the day, if you plan, you can create pick up and drop off times that benefit everyone.

Mothers are not perfect, and neither are we. Oh, Dearest, we have made our share of mistakes. You can forgive yourself and do better next time. Continually look for ways to improve. If you were late picking someone up, then leave earlier next time. If you have too many things on your plate, ask for others to help you for a while. Each member of a family or community can contribute for the benefit of all. They may need some convincing and even a little begging, but if you persevere, often people will offer their assistance.

While people often feel that they need to do everything by themselves, society is constructed so that we need one another. By asking for assistance when you need it, you will learn the abilities and strengths of others. Encourage rather than expect or force others to help you. They may not be willing because they do not feel comfortable with the task. Educate them about how to perform the duty and encourage anyone who helps with your work by thanking them and complementing them on what they do well. Encouragement will work ten times harder for you than discouragement. Use it to your advantage, Dear One.

Chapter Twelve
Death and Spirituality

The death of a loved one is one of the greatest pains that people face. We will lose loved ones. They and we rarely know when it is our time to go, so say kind things when you depart from loved ones until another day. If that was your last opportunity to say something to him or her, then at least you did it with caring. Living to have no regrets is something of great value. Do not do anything that you may regret later or that could produce unwanted consequences.

Grief is a difficult emotion and some people are not comfortable with us crying or speaking about our lost loved one. Do not let that make you think that it is unacceptable to cry or speak about them. Some people are not the right companion to share this aspect of your personality with, though they may care about you. Not everyone has been taught how to manage these deep emotions well. Other people may have had difficult or painful losses and your loss may remind them of something they do not wish to remember.

It is unfortunate that some people wish to forget their pain instead of feeling and understanding it. Our emotions serve a purpose and crying is a way that our body releases stress. Talking about our loved ones honors their memory and helps us organize our thoughts and feelings about her or him. We hope that people will remember us fondly one day, so why would we want others to forget their loved ones but remember us? Each life impacts many lives and even people who were mostly bad often showed concern or care about others. We may recall the deceased person's best moments, and the lessons we learned from their words and experience.

The death that hurts the most is when we lose someone who made our lives special and impacted us in a positive way. We wanted them to stay forever, but they could not. Some of us believe that our loved ones continue at a spiritual level. You may have similar beliefs or not. If you are a spiritual person, then worship may assist you through the process of letting go of your loved one and gradually moving forward. These things take time. Do not rush your grieving. That is not how you can resolve it in your mind.

Taking a negative and turning it into a positive is a way to deal with grief. You have lost someone and that may feel negative. You can do something positive about that, such as performing acts of kindness and compassion toward others in the memory of your loved one. What groups need your help? Or you may ask people you know if they would like your assistance with any projects. Another idea is listening to others and sharing caring.

Another coping skill for grief is creating something beautiful from your pain. People make memory books of their loved one's life to share with family and friends. You may journal about your best memories, plant a garden in their honor, create art that reminds you of them, compose a song about their impact on your life, or create other things. Many musicians have honored their loved one in song and then other people have appreciated listening to that song when they miss their departed one. Wealthy families often dedicate sections of a school or hospital for their loved ones, or create a scholarship in their name so that more students can attend college.

You may not always feel sad when someone dies, and some people feel guilt if they are happy someone has passed away. We should care about every human life, and yet, they may have hurt you or others. You may need time to release the pain and then put their humanity into perspective. Anger that we might harbor against someone who is deceased should be released, since there is no longer a possible resolution with him or her. They can no longer make it right with you. Tell your mind that you can do no more to make peace with him or her, so you will let it go. You may have to do that for weeks or months if the person has offended or hurt you. That is better than a lifetime of resentment.

If you are missing a loved one, the pain can be intense at first and over time is more manageable. If you were young, then you might have faint or lost memories about her or him and that happens to people, but you can still feel your love for them. What is important is that they existed and made a difference for you. In their honor, you can do wonderful things.

While I speak of times ahead, perhaps at this moment you are alone and missing a loved one terribly. The tears may be flowing, and it may feel like they will never stop. (((((HUG))))) We love you and wish you did not have to go through any pain. We have lost loved ones too and it is terrible. We will get through today. Tomorrow, we will plan to get through that day. People may feed us to show us love. They may visit with us out of compassion or they may stay away to respect your grief or pain. Eat if you feel like it and receive the company that visits. When you see the sunset, be thankful for another day away from that initial pain.

When you grieve, be kind with yourself and accepting. You may have little energy. You may not feel like doing things. It takes time to get over the shock of losing someone. You will not experience grief like anyone else, so be patient with others who may not understand and be thankful for anyone who cares enough about you to spend time with you during your time of need. When they need you or lose someone, you can return the favor. If not for them, then you can be there for someone else one day.

Darling, you will be okay and get through this. A minute at a time, then an hour at a time, then each day. We are here. The world awaits your recovery so that you can spread the love and your unique talents. Take care of your precious self for us. (((((HUG)))))

 # Anecdotes

Everything Will Be Okay

Dear Loved One,

There can be no greater pain than the loss of someone you

loved so dearly and there will be different phases you will go through. When we show our grief, remember, this is a testament of the love we felt for the ones we have lost and there are no right or wrong ways. When we lose someone we love so much, how can we not feel sad? From my own experience, I hope to help you through the process with what has helped me.

The first three years for me were the hardest; the pain was very raw. I speak of this in a singular tense because I lost two very dear people to me: my daughter and a granddaughter. I have lost others, but no pain has matched this one.

There are a few things that have helped me in the years since I lost them. Talking about them and keeping their memories alive has helped me. There was a time when all I could do was think about them, so I started writing down some of these memories and placing them in a special box. I call this my happy box. I think you will find as you start writing these memories down, more and more will come to mind. Over the years, I filled it with a mixture of happy and funny memories. On difficult days, go to that happy box, or whatever you decide to call it, shake the box up and keep pulling those memories out until you feel better. I think you will find that the deep sadness you were feeling will gradually turn to smiles and maybe even laughter. There will be times where you find yourself going to this box often and that is okay. Using the box is a good thing. Imagine how your loved one would feel, knowing that these precious times you shared together are so meaningful now, something that puts a smile back on your face. This is what I would want for my loved ones when my time has come.

Another thing I have done was not a conscious decision for me. I lost two very special people in a horrible tragedy and there were things about their deaths that I thought that if they had occurred differently, they would still be here with us, so I took these feelings and thoughts to my senator. When I left his office, it was with the understanding that a piece of legislation would be created to prevent something like this from happening to anyone else. It has been a long road—going on ten years now—and though we have made some headway, we haven't passed the legislation into law yet. I had times when I felt like giving up, but every time I do, something happens that gives me the hope that yes, this can be done, and back on the path I go again. If what I am doing can save just one life, their senseless deaths will be for something and oh, how proud they would be if their deaths were to save other lives! I like to think as well that their memories will live through the lives of possible victims and their families as well. So, here I am, nearly ten years later, ready to go another round. Now, I am not saying everyone should get legislation passed when a tragedy occurs, but if you can find a passion for something, you might be surprised at how this helps you, even if you become an advocate for something your loved one felt so much passion for.

The most important message I want to give you, Darling, is be kind to yourself. Know what you are feeling is not only normal, but it is okay. It is okay to shed those tears. They can be very healing to us. Don't let yourself bottle up all that love you had. Don't you think there will be people in your life that will do the same for you when your time comes?

If I could give you a great big hug right now and tell you

that things will be okay, this is what I would do. I hope you embrace this love I'm sending you.

The Beautiful Pearl

I visited the crematorium today to see where my sister's ashes have been interred (she died a few months ago). I was very close to her and she was my best friend. My dad's ashes are interred very near to hers. He died thirty years ago when I was twenty-four. Both deaths have left a huge gap in my heart.

Dear Friend, if you are experiencing grief right now, how I'd love to put my arms around you and comfort and reassure you. Grieving a loved one is not an easy thing and at some stage in our lives we will all experience it. Grief is such a unique experience for each person. Don't worry if your grief doesn't look like others' around you but try not to ignore the pain or bottle it up. There is no set time frame for grief, either. You will move through the grieving process in your own time and in your own way. Be kind to yourself. Give yourself the time and space you need. It's okay to set boundaries but try not to push everyone away. Grief can be such a complicated and conflicting thing. Sometimes you want people around you and sometimes you just want to be left alone. Being alone for a while can give you the space to reflect and to work through your feelings. At times, you may need to reminisce and feel comforted by the memories. At other times, you may need to do the work of forgiving—both others and you—in order to not get stuck.

I pray that there are people in your life that can bring you comfort, but the truth is that no matter how many people are there for you, grief is a very lonely experience. You must go through the loneliness and pain of it because if you try to avoid it, the process will only be delayed. The key is to realize that it *is a process,* and you will come out the other side. You will get through this and come into better days! Not only that, but you will become a better person too—more caring and understanding of others' pain; and that is a very valuable gift to give someone. Try to receive the comfort in whatever form it comes to you. Allow yourself to be cared for and loved by others, even if their efforts are somewhat clumsy at times.

You might never know *why* your loved ones had to go and it's futile to get caught up in trying to reason it out, but you can make decisions for your life that will honor their memory and give hope to others.

I hope that this dream, which I had not long after my father passed away, will bring comfort to you as it has to me:

I walked into our kitchen and my father was standing there. I was shocked to see him alive again and I asked him why he was here. He answered that he'd come back to give me this, and I looked down to see that he'd placed something in my hand. It was a beautiful white pearl.

Pearls are beautiful things and each one is unique. Pearls are usually created in a closed shell at the bottom of the ocean. This gave me hope that, no matter how dark and lonely I felt inside, something beautiful was going to be created inside of me despite all the pain.

Stay in the process, Dear Friend, and allow that pain to shape you, because one day you and everyone will see *the beautiful pearl* that you have become.

© 2019 Jill Magnussen, "The Beautiful Pearl"

Part Two

A Father's Heart

Introducing the delight of the heart
of boys and men

We Are Your Family: One Love, One Family

Dear Beautiful Soul, each one of us is different in a special way, and for a special reason. We are all created with love, and each one of us has a purpose on Earth. Regardless of where you come from, what you look like, or who your family is, you have an important role, and the secret in life is to find it. But finding your role and purpose begins with finding the love you were created with, searching deep within your soul where it waits for you. It's when you find this gift within that you flourish, and your self-esteem grows.

If you compare yourself to others and believe that what they say or think is normal, then you will never grow the way you should. Understand that there are millions of other people in this world like you. They are experiencing everything you are, were raised exactly like you, and can relate to everything in your life, but they have a very high self-esteem. So why is it that they do, and you perhaps don't? It starts with believing in yourself and accepting who you are. Accept every single thing about yourself and understand that this is what makes you the special and the unique person that you are meant to be. When you become vulnerable, you accept things in an entirely different manner, and your inner love grows.

If I could give you one gift that would change the rest of your life, it would be the gift of self-love. I don't believe there is anything better than achieving this, and when you do, your life and self-esteem will flourish more than you can imagine. But you will never find it if you keep comparing yourself to others, listening to your ego instead of your heart, and staying focused on your past with consistent negative thinking.

Start by looking in the mirror and telling yourself, "I love you." Tell yourself all the reasons why, and comment on everything you feel is a fault with an "I love you because—." You will soon learn that there are no faults; never were, and you are exactly who you were meant to be. That is the magic that transforms. Remember, your mind is your biggest enemy. Retrain it to think positive thoughts. If you feed it with good things, it will hold onto those and replay them, eventually replacing the negative.

It took me forty-six years to accept who I was and love myself. I believed that I was an outcast, a failure, and would never be happy in my life, no matter how hard I fought my mental illness. I have severe anxiety and panic disorder. I was physically and mentally abused when I was younger, and it resulted in developing in post-traumatic stress disorder, or PTSD. So, you can understand why it took me so long to build up my self-esteem and find love for myself. My anxiety causes everything positive in my mind to turn negative if I allow it.

When I became vulnerable, I learned there were millions just like me, that it was okay to be me, and that others could relate to everything I was sharing. This was when I saw a positive change, and my heart grew again. I had to accept what happened to me when I was younger, accept that, yes, I was different but for a reason, and focus everything on the love in my heart, putting full trust in that love. I changed my routine. I woke up with the sunrise and gave thanks for every new beautiful day. I read positive things and focused on things that made me happy. Consistently, I said "I love you" every time I looked in the mirror. I shared everything about myself with the people close to me and put everything on the table. There were no secrets, nothing else to reveal. This was who I am, and I loved myself more every day. Instantly, my self-esteem grew and my outlook on not only myself, but life and how I lived it improved. Love for myself and others was surreal. And, most importantly, I discovered my purpose. It changed my life.

A higher self-esteem comes with vulnerability, inner focus, consistent reinforcement of thoughts from your heart (not focus on what others say), and the belief that you were created for a reason. It can only come from true heartfelt love for yourself. For some, it takes shutting off the outside world and being at one with yourself to hear the call of your heartbeat. If it takes silence, then find it. Only you have control over your mind and the choices you make, and this is important to remember. There is a saying: "What you think about, you bring about." For me, this is exactly what I did for most of my life; all I did was replay my past and keep a negative mindset, so that is exactly what came into my life and kept my self-esteem so low.

Our mind is a fascinating thing, and the hardest thing people face is controlling it. It takes a lot of practice and time, but with consistency, you can do it. Recognize anything that makes you unhappy. Every time you find yourself replaying something negative, replace that thought with a positive one. Your mind is your computer. You decide what is uploaded into it, and you can delete any files you want from it to the trash bin. Declutter and defrag it regularly, and you will soon see the power behind it.

You are a beautiful creation. You are loved, you are special, and you are a wonderful gift that all the world is grateful for. Live your life for you, not everyone else. Listen to your heart. Be kind, be grateful, and compare yourself to no one. Spend your time doing things that make you happy and do those things as much as you can. Live for today and keep your focus on today and making it the best you can. Let go of yesterday. You can't change anything about it, so let it free.

Love yourself. Be proud of the amazing being that you are and give gratitude anytime you can. Be patient for things. If you are meant to have them, they will come into your life. Self-esteem is something that you build over time, and with that self-esteem comes character, strength, and integrity.

Your heart and your mind are the two most important gifts you were given. Always put your heart first, and your mind second.

Your Family is larger than you will ever know, and the deeper love you find within will bring a better understanding of this. We are all one, and it is the love within our hearts that binds us all together. That is why leading with your heart is of such importance. Doing so will direct you on your path, and it is your footprints left behind you that will leave an imprint on everyone, forever. It's not how many steps you take in life, but the depth of each one. Some of you will become parents; your children and their children will follow those very footsteps, so walk gently.

For men, this may be more difficult, since we are considered the strong role model. A man's true strength is not just physical, but spiritual. Strength is built through courage, and as a male, it will take great courage to let go of all stereotypes about whom and what you are supposed to be, and to learn to listen to your heart. You will gather more strength there than you can ever imagine. It will bring kindness, honesty, sincerity, and gentleness, along with so many things that are relevant for understanding others. Women and children need this side of a man; it's this side they relate with, and it is this side that will always be an important piece of their hearts.

We are all family, every one of us. Much love, Dear One. I wish you a beautiful life.

© 2019 Todd Sarsons (Budokaizen), "We Are Your Family: One Love, One Family"

Chapter Thirteen
Choosing a Career Path

You Are Your Destiny

Loved One, a career path is filled with a life of purpose. So, how do we choose? How do we commit to something which is lifelong? The answer is finding something you are passionate about. As they say, "If you love what you do, you won't ever do a day's work again!" Whatever your passion is, whether it's painting, music, or writing, do that every day, and forge your own career! If you are a painter, you may not have access to the finest materials. All you need to do is pick up a pen or pencil and make your masterpiece. If your passion is music, just start. You may not have a musical instrument, but can you sing? Does someone have an instrument you can borrow and use? Can you read a book on how to read music? Have a big vision for your career but start small. The concept is to take an action every day that helps you toward the career that you would love. Can you study others that you admire? Can you read their books? Study their life stories and read their biographies? Loved One, use your creative mind and you will find a way.

The important thing here, Loved One, is that there are no fixed rules. You may love music and then fall out of love with it. That's okay! You can still choose something else. You may think there are rules for defining your career, but even now, mine is evolving and changing depending on my evolution; remember, you will evolve too, and you too may change. If you practice your passion and love the thing that you do each day, you will build a career that is unique for you.

You may ask, what if I am not able to start straight away? Perhaps I have to do something or earn some money to do the thing that I love! That's okay too. Sometimes, we must do things that we don't enjoy, but this may be the path we take to enable us to do the thing we love. This is called DISCIPLINE. Don't look at discipline as something to be avoided. Discipline is training when things become difficult and is a great teacher. She will teach you RESILIENCE, which is another amazing quality when things get difficult. Resilience makes you get stronger from doing what is not easy and to not quit.

You may be having a difficult time now, and by learning discipline and building resilience, you will prepare yourself for a career that will be amazing. Every career will have its own challenges and you need to be prepared to face them. Everyone who has had a career they love has found it difficult. Just like you read in Chapter One, the people that forged their careers did so out of these deep and looked-for qualities. The path to their chosen career was not well trodden and they had to make their own way. With things like the Internet and books, we can study their path and take onboard the lessons they have learned so you can build your career in your own unique way.

Many people believe that they should settle for a safe and okay career, but stretching yourself, speaking to people who are doing the thing you would love to do, is the first step to making your career happen. You may say, "But I don't know anyone here that is in a career I love." As previously said, use a book and the Internet if it's available to you. Remember, that was the path others took and you need to carve your own. Following a career of passion is difficult, because it takes commitment, dedication, and a lot of hard work. Sometimes, you will feel that you have been put off course. In reality, you are doing what you must do as training for you to access the next step of your career.

Seek people out; ask if you can work for them and see what it would be like in the industry that you choose. When you are selecting what you would love to do for the rest of your life, it is important to try lots of different things to make sure that you will enjoy something. Remember, Loved One, there are no set rules. Go with what you feel is right for you. You are UNIQUE. The people around you do not know you deep down, only you do. You need to listen to that voice inside that comes from the heart that says, "If I could do this for the rest of my life, then every day would be filled with joy and purpose, and I would be living a full life on my terms!"

Always keep your mind sharp, Loved One. Stay creative. If you choose a career, find a new way to deliver it into existence. Use your imagination. What would be the best version of that career in your mind? What would make it unique to you? It could be a career in an already established business or you could create your own business! Don't let anyone take your imagination and creativity away from you. Some may say you are a dreamer. People who say this have already lost faith in their dreams. Do not let this be you! I had similar people around me. You know what you want to do and sometimes the path is lonely, but if you have developed RESILIENCE, DISCIPLINE, and BELIEF, you will succeed in the end.

When you are struggling, make sure that your environment is filled with INSPIRATION and BELIEF. If you admire someone, try and obtain a photo or something they have written to keep you motivated and inspired through the difficult times. People who have pursued successful careers have had difficult times and they have pushed through with the belief that they can make it happen. One thing you can do is imagine you were 80 or 90 years old and you look back on your life. Would you regret not going for the career you would have loved? The good news is that you are not there yet and you can take those actions now!

Remember, Loved One, it is possible to have the career of your dreams. Be dedicated, resilient, disciplined, and work harder than anyone else to make it happen. You are enough and you are committed to developing the skills and locating the tools to make it happen. Stay INSPIRED!

© 2019 Joe Noya, "You Are Your Destiny"

Anecdotes

Wisdom to Build a House

We need to be very careful choosing our career path. Orphans struggle too much in life and many of us fail to make the full meaning of the purpose in our hearts for this world. We fail to reach our visions, goals and dreams. This mostly happens when we do not accept who we are. We become confused by not being content with what we have.

Afflictions will be there, but they make us strong enough to encounter challenges; they are for a moment. You may think you need money to build a house. I think you need wisdom to do it, because it's through wisdom that the house is built.

Just like a dog remembers someone who has always attended to it, the habit of our hard work in school helps prepare us to make better decisions. You were given a mind to make good or bad decisions. The power of making your own choices depends on you. No one can decide for you what to do unless you agree. Every decision you make has consequences, whether good or bad, and you can hurt those who love you to please those who don't deserve you. Most of the solutions for our problems come from us. The answers are always within us.

Reflect on your thinking by observing what you see in your environment. Think about your old age, when you won't have enough strength, when you will not have the ability to see clearly. How will you survive without investing? How will you invest if you don't work hard? How will you work hard if you don't accept who you are?

Trying a different thing takes courage and promotes us to the next level. Without that, you shall remain in the same or an even worse situation. The journey of success is to start something new.

© *2019 George Omondi Owiti, "Wisdom to Build a House"*

Chapter Fourteen
From Boy to Man

From a Boy into a Man

In the past, people believed that money was the source of happiness. It is not totally wrong. Especially because in earlier times, not many people were educated. Their insights about life were narrow and shallow. But as many people became more educated everywhere, science and technology rapidly advanced, and the world became smaller through the widespread use of the Internet. The perspective on happiness has also shifted. It is no longer money that makes happiness, but rather, happiness that makes money.

To put it more precisely, happiness makes the quality of service and friendship with others much better. Happiness makes your smile much brighter. Happiness transforms your daily life into a temple of love. As a result, money comes to you more easily—especially because customers can easily trust you. Employers fall in love with your qualities. Friends and family will see you as their source of light. The trust of people can be an infinite source of fortunes. For these reasons, it is highly recommended to learn happiness deeply.

As contemplative material, nowadays, happiness is the most wanted medicine. It is the energy that drives human beings to grow and glow and the motivation that makes people wake up in the morning in high spirits. Even the United Nations has made a happiness index among countries for the last ten years. In short, in our world today, happiness is a nutrition both for the body and the soul. In other words, it is worth making your soul grow by using happiness as the path. As you grow older, you will know that happiness is both the path and the end of the journey.

Sources of happiness

In soul evolution, there are three sources of happiness. In the beginning, the source of happiness is giving something to yourself, from buying new clothes, to eating delicious chocolate. It is understandable, since this is just the beginning of the journey. All teenagers and spiritual beginners experience this kind of happiness—being happy by giving something to yourself. It makes the body healthier, the mind more peaceful, and the heart more thankful.

As the body grows older, and the soul grows much more mature, this kind of happiness is no longer adequate. By that time, the second source of happiness appears, especially being happy by making others happy. It is like the love of a mother to her only baby. When the mother buys new clothes for the only baby, the baby knows nothing about the new clothes, but the mother who gave them to the baby is deeply happy. The same thing happens to a mature soul. The source of happiness is no longer getting something but giving something.

The impact of this second, deeper kind of happiness to the quality of your service and friendship with others will be much more profound. People will feel something positively different about you. Respect and praise easily flows to you. Trust will grow from time to time. At the end, more money comes to you. You can be rich both outside and inside. The way you walk and grow in daily life will be uniquely different.

The third, and the deepest source of happiness is inner contentment. Not because you stop working, studying, or praying. Again, it isn't. But you begin to understand through attainment, that everything is the dancing of the same perfection. Failure and success are like night and day that keep flowing every day.

In this stage, happiness is no longer a destination. It is the journey itself. In every step, there is happiness. While ordinary people look outside for it, at this stage, happiness can be found inside as something natural. Happiness is as natural as a beautiful flower and the birds that sing with gratitude. As a result, your smile will be full of light. Your service will be very touching. This evolution is not only from a boy into a man, but also how an ordinary soul evolves into an enlightened soul.

© 2019 Guruji Gede Prama, "From a Boy into a Man"

Guruji Gede Prama is a meditation facilitator in the island of love: Bali, Indonesia.

Chapter Fifteen
Work Ethics

What Is Work Ethic?

I expect you're wondering what it is to have a good work ethic. But there's a huge difference between knowing what it is and showing you have one. Now the good news! I'll show you that whatever a Good Work Ethic is, you're doing a lot of it already! And, you can do it better if you practice. Plus, if there's something you're not doing, you can learn to do it.

So, let's go on a short journey—one you've travelled many times before. But this time, we're going to focus on what you do without thinking. You do it automatically and it has become a habit.

A journey

Imagine you've planned to meet your friends for a special occasion. It could be for a celebration, maybe a party, perhaps to watch your favourite team or maybe something else.

This special occasion means a lot to you and you're excited and enthusiastic. Now, I bet you'll say "yes" to all the following in this list:

- You're dressed ready for action! You look great, feel great and smell great!
- You'll be there on time so as not to miss anything.
- You'll have planned getting there by bus, coach, taxi or car. Maybe you have coordinated and negotiated with a friend to catch a ride.
- When you get there, you'll have a great attitude, chatting, laughing, smiling and helping everyone have a great time. You may not be the centre of attention, but you'll be you and do your thing.
- You'll be a great friend and supportive of your mates, making sure no one is miserable or left behind.
- You'll be having fun and letting your real character shine. After all, your friends are friends because they like you too!
- If there's any sort of issue, you'll sort it out as any good team player would and speak out if you think there's a better way.

So, be honest, did you say yes? If you did, you're well on your way to not only understanding what a good work ethic is, but you've got what it takes to do it.

Fake News—the beliefs about what employers want

When I was teenager at school, my teachers would say, "Get good qualifications, Neville, and you're guaranteed to get a good job." They believed they were right and telling me the truth, but unfortunately, it was not only #fakenews then, some

50 years later, I can tell you that nothing has changed—it's still #fakenews.

> *"Your technical skills account for 15% of your success*
> *—85% of your success is from your attitude*
> *and soft skills."*
>
> Dale Carnegie Foundation

Qualifications do count, but employers want to employ people who have a good work ethic. By now, I hope you'll realise that's simply having a can-do attitude and good soft skills. They want to hire people that turn up ready for work, are able listen to instruction, can communicate, work with others, and do their best to improve themselves and help the organisation succeed. And yes, they pay you to turn up and do the job!

Again, all of these you should have said "yes" to above.

Make the link

Employers know you are not going to do the job perfectly on Day 1. They have a recruitment process that includes an interview to weed out those with a bad attitude and poor soft skills. At the interview, they will see everything you said "yes" to above, from turning up smart and on time, to showing you can listen and talk with a can-do attitude.

If you can now make the link for yourself, you will leapfrog ahead and what's more, you will never look back. You can now start thinking about what you need to improve. When you do,

I have two pieces of advice that will help you to raise your awareness and get better.

"If you think you can do something, or you think you can't then you're right!"
Henry Ford, creator of the Model T Ford Motorcar

"Listen to think, not to respond."
Neville Gaunt, Chairman and architect of Your Passport2Grow

Now here's a list that employers will recognise as part of a Good Work Ethic:

1. Appearance: is dressed appropriately, is well-groomed, has good hygiene, and good manners.
2. Attendance: arrives and leaves on time, meets deadlines, and plans all leave with the boss.
3. Attitude: shows a can-do attitude, appears confident, committed and has self-belief.
4. Character: displays loyalty, honesty, dependability, reliability, initiative, and self-control.
5. Communication: listens and displays proper verbal and non-verbal skills.
6. Cooperation: displays leadership skills; properly handles criticism, conflicts, and stress; maintains proper relationships with peers and follows chain of command.
7. Organizational Skill: shows skills in managing time, prioritizing, and dealing with change.

8. Productivity: follows safety practices, conserves resources, and follows instructions.
9. Respect: deals properly with diversity, shows understanding and tolerance.
10. Teamwork: respects others, works well in teams, is helpful, confident, displays a customer service attitude, and wants to learn.

Pick one skill you want to improve—google it and see how others get good at it. Then, go and do something yourself. The only way to get a good work ethic (be a good friend) is to go and practice.

If I can help more, check out www.YP2Grow.com, as there are lots of answers to many of your questions.

© 2020 Neville Gaunt, "What Is Work Ethic?"

 # Anecdotes

Caring, Fatherly Advice on Work

Hello. I'm a Dad to two daughters, and I want to give you some helpful advice on work, as any kind, caring and compassionate parent would for their own child.

This will help you in broader life as well as at work. Once in work, you need to find folk who do these things, or help folk who need them.

These are "soft" people skills that we can put under the heading of teamwork. We all need to work with others, at home, in corporate roles, and increasingly, in a world staring at the tricky prospect of automation. These skills may also support a growing incidence in networking settings, where independent business folk need rapid ways to find out what is valuable to the individual they are talking with, and to join their team. Teamwork has always been a fantastic and attractive characteristic, but it is now becoming essential in the working world.

In fact, in corporations, a really good leader will seek out these attitudes and values in people he or she works with and seek to help such aligned folk work more broadly with others.

What every caring parent wants for their child is **independence, resilience in the face of difficulty, and a caring disposition** toward others. Putting these soft skills at the heart of teamwork gives us very strong foundations.

A caring disposition means that children can pass on good family values as they are able, however difficult their own starting point in life.

A caring parent wants independence for their child because in time, the child must stand on their own two feet, and the parent will become less able to help, through age or infirmity.

And a loving parent cannot stand to see a child suffer. Having resilience means that a child will still at times suffer, but over time, will have resourcefulness and an ability to find means and ways to ease that suffering for themselves.

Bosses are no different from parents here. An **independent employee** can go off and work on a specific task without needing excessive oversight and guidance. A **resilient employee** can take the inevitable knock backs that life and work frequently put in our paths. And a **compassionate employee** can support other employees. A boss may often be juggling multiple tasks and be very grateful that team support can be delegated to another member of staff.

How do parents, or caring adults, support a child's journey, before and during work?

Wise guides (I'll share more on that later on) tell us there are three causes of suffering to be vigilant about, namely ignorance, greed and hatred.

Ignorance causes suffering because we are unable to see ways ahead when we are stuck. Life can throw up difficult situations. **Greed** causes suffering when we hoard resources, materials and wealth to ourselves, and deprive others. **Hatred** causes suffering because folk actively harm others, by deed or by word.

We all need to **be vigilant against these tendencies in ourselves**, throughout our lives, because sometimes we don't see the impact we have on others. It's one aspect of our ignorance.

How do we become vigilant about our impact on ourselves and others?

Our whole lives, education is the way we tackle ignorance. Knowledge in the world is limitless, so we need to recognise learning is lifelong. By learning, we can make sure we can acquire and maintain independence and resilience, so we are strong enough to help others when they need it. Educational systems are generally not that perfect, so we must take it on ourselves to be responsible for our own education, during and way beyond school. The Internet is a huge learning resource and can be used for great good.

Tackling greed is about understanding sufficiency. When do we have enough, and when can we help others? Too many people think the way to help others is by acquiring a lot of money, so they can spend it and spread wealth. But the real key is in gaining valuable employment that generates value for others. This can be through farming, fishing, and yes, even through finance. If we all had creating value as a focus, instead of simply earning money, the world would be a far better place.

Wise sages tell us it's right that everyone in the world wants to be happy. Indeed, that we are entitled to be happy.

But that's not always easy. Some folk only focus on their own happiness, and their own wealth. That over focus can be at the expense of others and can even cause others suffering.

The antidote for this selfishness is compassion. We can **develop and nurture ways to care for others**, through small actions, through consoling words, and more if we are able. We can show that we care for all our fellow human beings, no matter how different from us they may be.

The final human tendency we must be vigilant for is hatred.

When folk are deeply hurt, an ancient instinct in humans is to protect ourselves. Animal genetics tells us that fright, flight or fight are instinctive reactions to dangerous or difficult situations.

None of these are helpful. As sentient humans, **we have a duty to grow beyond these animal instincts**, and we do have innate abilities to understand more and behave better.

Fright means that we are frozen, unable to act to change a situation. **Flight** means we run away from the situation, which remains unchanged, and still needs to be tackled. And **fight** means we risk harming another person, possibly causing them pain, and leaving them with wounds they may then respond to with their own animal instincts.

We really must do better than simply giving in to our animal instincts.

A good way to do this is to try to understand why folk give us the angry, hurt responses they sometimes do.

We are all human, and we are all also still those instinctive animals. Most often, we can rise above our animal instincts. But on occasion, **if we are tired, upset, unwell, stuck, or angry**, we may revert to our animal instincts. But there is almost always that reason, a suffering, and some are buried very deeply. If we can understand the suffering, then we can respond differently to difficult behaviours.

I've tried to encapsulate and summarise many things I've learned as a parent. It's what I want for my children, and I hope it also has some value for you!

At work, a good leader would treat all their staff, in fact anyone they came into contact with, as extended members of their family. A good leader will want to help their team grow, whatever their starting points. Not all leaders are created equally, however, and good leaders are rare enough that loyal workers tend to follow them from job to job.

Hopefully, this might help you choose which leaders to follow, and perhaps when to change direction.

To understand more about finding paths to freedom from suffering, and understanding ignorance, greed and hatred as causes of suffering, do read the Twitter stream and writings of HH The Dalai Lama. The Dalai Lama is recognised as a great spiritual leader, mainly for his **highly pragmatic and common-sense approach to living happily, compassionately and securely.**

Please do understand the world is a big mixture of folk. Many are hurt and suffering. Some visibly, some not. Other folk have set themselves to the task of being kind, caring and compassionate to their fellow human beings. Honestly, these kind souls do exist, and you can find them on the Internet, even if there are none physically near to where you live.

Your job with everyone you meet is to see whether they are that kind, compassionate person, or whether **perhaps you are the stronger one**, and they actually need your help! Finding ways to assist can be a challenge; sometimes there is a strong need for subtlety. Many folk are embarrassed to ask for help, but all of us should always aim to be humble enough to ask for it when we need it. This humility would be a big help toward harmonious human relationships.

Age doesn't matter. Gender doesn't matter. Culture doesn't matter. We are united in our capacity for suffering as human beings.

So, we really do need to be kind and caring toward one another. And that way, together, we will make a better world.

Remember, **if you seek help, you are much more likely to find it.** Good luck!

© *2019 Peter Jones, "Caring, Fatherly Advice on Work"*

Chapter Sixteen
Finances

Family Financing with Love

There are many models for financial planning used by families. However, they seem to fall into these categories: austerity, strict budgeting, rainy day planning, free-for-all, or financing with love. Financial planning with love gives children a happy and healthy home.

Financing with love is to provide wisely and make a good life the emphasis, rather than to use financial formulas.

The other methods—and the many combinations and variations thereof—are designed with an over-emphasis or under-emphasis on money. With our theme, the priority of family is love. Love creates a home, maintains the home and nurtures children. Not money. Of course, for love to accomplish this, many things are necessary, and money is one of those ingredients. It is neither evil nor a golden goal. It is an ingredient, to be handled wisely and in the right amounts.

I have met some not unhappy parents who are constantly consumed with checking the bottom line. I have also met unhappy parents who point to a budget as sacrosanct. There are those who plan for some possible "rainy day" which may never come, with no idea of how much that would cost in present circumstances or how much could be needed on that day. Of course, those who give no thought at all to finances are like chefs who do not know which ingredients are poured into the pot and how much is left for the next customer.

Planning and budgeting are important in keeping a home on a sound footing. Income and expenses need to be balanced. There is no responsible real estate management or financing firm that would allow renters or buyers to spend too much of their income flow on monthly housing costs. There is no financing available for a company that does not have a sound basis for the spending of that financing.

Like a real estate firm, a family needs to balance overall monthly expenses against present (not future) income flow. Like the financing institution, a family needs to see that the overall expenditure is designed to produce the best product. What is a family's *product*? It is love and the nurturing of the family—with an emphasis on children. There is growth in the family *business*, as the children of the day will be the adults of the future. Properly financed, they will expand the *franchise* in the best possible way.

I have been chided by friends for not sweating the details on a receipt for small purchases. They are right, I do not. We are given a very limited amount of time to provide for children. Time is an ingredient in the equation that we cannot control. We can, however, manage our time spent versus our unknown time income stream. My financial advice, as a father, grandfather—and MBA—is to spend your time as generously as possible on love and family. Receipts are usually on small pieces of paper and are mostly small in context and reward.

Time is best spent on not penny-pinching, haggling or combing through the small monetary issues.

The ingredients for love and family need to be used in balance and proportion. Time spent on love and family is the wisest economic use of those valuable ingredients.

The ingredient of money is important, but only as a component. The big picture is most appropriate for that ingredient, which is seeing the overall budgeting in tracking income flow versus expenditure. The primary needs for the family are foremost: a proper home, health needs, food, clothing, insurance and education. These are the big items. Money for these must be adequately provided for, so that the family and the products that the family needs are produced. Anything drawing from the primary needs that causes potential for the family income-expenditure ratio to be harmed needs to be checked immediately.

Serious issues can affect a healthy family income-expenditure ratio. Addictions of any sort can lead to a terrible drain on income. Envy—ranging from keeping up with the Joneses to current fashion "needs" can be a source of another. These are big picture issues that, if not checked, become a crisis that can change a loving home.

However, that does not mean you need to live with a pencil behind your ear and a calculator in your hand. It does not mean keeping a child from something because of some small perceived expense. Do not become the person who likes to check the store receipt over and over. Time is the unknown expense-to-value ratio that is spent on such petty acts.

Love and children need a responsible blend of ingredients to grow. Be responsible but keep your eye on the prize.

Anecdotes

Manage Your Money—Manage Your Future

Finances are a subject nobody ever seems to want to talk about. Yet, dear friends, they are probably the most important thing to build a foundation in, so that you have the strength and the ability to do other things, including helping others on your journey through life.

You don't have to be rich to be attractive or happy. Money doesn't make you shine inside, my friends. However, good money management reduces stress and eliminates arguments with those close to you, and not owing people money puts you in better control of your own destiny.

If anyone ever tries to sit down and talk to you about money, immediately you become defensive and pretend that you know everything about money, so you rarely pay attention. This is a very normal reaction. Now is your opportunity to stop being normal; be different. Absorb this information and make it work for you. I promise, that even without a formal education, working hard and managing your money correctly will set you up for continued success in life. This is not one of those, "Look at me and how I made a million dollars" sales or bragging about things that are unachievable for ninety-nine percent of the population. This is from someone who left school without the qualifications, went to work, and saw how working hard at your chosen field, be it in art, labor, administration or educating yourself, was a key part of being successful in life.

After twenty years of earning money and looking forward to each paycheck as though it were Christmas, I finally learned to say, "No!" I began saving money and planning for things. I started only spending money I had put to one side for that event. Instead of waking up the day after a vacation worrying about paying a credit card, I had the money to spend saved up prior to the vacation. Ironically as I sit writing this, I am between jobs. I am not panicking because when I worked, I saved up a fund that would give me a six-month cushion for just such an event. If you save it up and never need it, just think of the fun you can have, or the people you can help. This advice applies if you're a pop star, a banker, a boxer (ask Mike Tyson), or a hard-working laborer.

I've heard of plenty of famous people making and losing millions, simply because they didn't pay attention to their own money, and I've seen such happiness and success in a married father of three, simply because, although he might only make enough to pay the mortgage and run two used vehicles, he has no debt other than his mortgage, and he has two thousand dollars cash in a safe in his house for emergencies. The simplicity of that makes him feel like a king. Whatever his wife and family want he can provide, and if they want something he can't afford to buy, he either says, "We can't afford it!" or, "We will have to save up for it!"

People want things and buy them on credit. There's

nothing wrong with wanting things, but the correct way is to save up and have the cash for your purchase or a sizeable deposit on large items, so that if you have to sell the item as used you can at least sell it for enough to pay off the financing.

Let's look at an example: purchasing a car for $10,000, without any deposit and an interest rate of six percent. A dealer will add tax and fees, so you will probably end up financing somewhere in the region of $11,500. Your monthly payment over four years will be around $269, paying a total of $12,912 over four years. In that time, you will have paid interest of around $1,500. If you have $3,000 as a down payment, you will significantly reduce your monthly payment to around $199 a month and save almost $400 on total interest. If you can't save $3,000, lower your sights and save $1,000. Just remember to lower the price of your target vehicle. A funny thing happens when you start to save; you like it, it's contagious and you want to save more.

Once, I was asked to be a co-signer. I asked the person who needed a co-signer to qualify for credit, "Why won't they let you sign?" The reply was, "I don't have good credit." I paused for a while and said, "If you had saved up, even a small portion of each paycheck, even 10 percent of each check, you would not be asking me for help." Their answer is my favorite finance reply, "That's what I normally do!" Everyone says that, except, that's exactly what they never have done.

It's all habit. Good habits become a ritual to success; bad

habits hold you back. No! I didn't co-sign. I did sit and show them how to plan money, even while on low income.

You work to earn money for you, not to pay the credit card man in his flashy car, or the new car dealership man. Earn your money and plan your money: short-term, a week to two weeks—even daily if necessary—annually, mid-term, and long-term. This means that when you get paid, you know that you need rent, auto, food, and utilities for two weeks. You also know over the year that you will need money to pay for clothes, birthdays, holidays and auto repairs. Long-term, you might want a vacation, marriage, house, and to care for a family. Write some numbers down and work backwards.

For holidays and clothes, for example, saving $40 a paycheck in one year can give you over $1,000 set aside to spend as you please. Save an extra $5 a paycheck and you have a nice $130 for a birthday splash or two. Plan and stick to it, and never be afraid to say, "No, I can't do that right now. It's not in my budget!"

Years ago, I stopped using my debit card and credit card and I started putting money into different categories of cash. For clothes, it was $40 a paycheck. After a few months, I went to the drawer where I had put the money, and just for clothes I had $240. I felt like a king walking around the local clothes store with $240 cash and buying anything I wanted—such a turnaround from waiting until my paycheck came and wondering if I could spend something on clothes that week. And I'm basically a jeans and T-shirt person. In fact, I remember I only ever had two pair of jeans, the ones I would wear and the ones in the washing machine. Now if I go on vacation, I feel sad for the jeans I leave behind. To this day, on payday, I take $160 cash and put it in my wallet, so if I am asked to do anything unplanned, such as a friends' night out, etc., it must come out of that. If I don't have the cash, I don't do it. It's a good habit and one I won't change.

© *2019 Gerard McAlroy, "Manage Your Money—Manage Your Future"*

Chapter Seventeen
Understanding Men

Communicating with Men

Compared with many of the subjects addressed here, this topic is simple. To communicate with men, start with the things that interest them. Once again, this is quite simple. In order of importance, men are interested in:

1. Women
2. Food
3. Sports

Occasionally, based on the time of day and maybe the season, some of these items can and will change position. In the fall, for example, football can move to the number one position with food and women falling completely off their radar. Sometimes, with no warning at all, food can move to the top of the list and stay there for as long as it takes to make a quick trip to the refrigerator or McDonald's.

Men are relatively easy to understand once you know how they are motivated. Communicating with this sex becomes very simple as long as you begin any conversation with one of the three subjects.

For example, girls, if you would like to talk to a boy about your feelings, start off with something like this: "Boy, how about those Cowboys this weekend? It was quite a game, huh?"

Initially, you might only receive a grunt in response, but you have at least gotten his attention. At this point, try mentioning another one of the three subjects with something such as, "And did you see the cheerleaders?"

If you still don't have his attention, you can pull out all the stops and say, "Hey, I am going to make a sandwich. Would you like one?"

You are almost certainly guaranteed that he will make eye contact with you at this point, and respond with, "Huh?"

Now, you can ask him the question that you have on your mind.

To go a little deeper into the subject of how to communicate with men, you must also understand their thought process. It is an understatement to say that girls and boys and men and women approach thinking differently . . . and that is part of the fun and part of the attraction to the opposite sex. Besides all the obvious differences between males and females, guys go about making decisions, communicating, and listening in an approach foreign to girls and women.

Guys think more linearly, or in a line. Whether we like it or not, we think more by going down a "check list" and we answer our check list questions in terms of yes or no. This process has worked well for men for thousands of years.

Our female counterpoints have a much more complicated thought process. They look at things from a wider variety of viewpoints than we do (and feelings come into play in a big way).

It is no surprise that guys have no trouble talking with other guys, and girls can talk for hours to other girls effortlessly. It gets a little more complicated when the two sexes try communicating with each other.

The art of conversation between men and women and boys and girls has been a source of joy, confusion, and frustration since the beginning of time. I feel quite sure that Adam and Eve struggled to understand each other. The first time Eve asked, "Does this leaf make me look fat?" I'll bet Adam responded, "You look *fine*," without looking up from his dinner. From that point on, there has been trouble in paradise.

Thousands of years later, males and females still struggle to be understood. Both sexes desperately want the same thing . . . to share their likes, dreams and passions with others. We want others to know how we feel, and to share experiences . . . and in a nutshell to be heard!

Problems arise when one or both people try so hard to be heard that they forget to listen. You may have heard the saying that communication is a two-way street. It is so true, but it is also so very hard to do. Many of us spend so much time in conversation thinking about what *we* are going to say next, that we completely ignore what the other one is saying. If the other person is doing the same thing, then there is no communication.

My father, who was a very wise man, would always tell me, "If you will just listen, you can learn something from everyone you speak to." He had rich friends and poor friends. Some of his friends had never been to school and others were highly educated. He knew doctors and lawyers and had many friends who were unemployed, but he listened to them all. More importantly, he listened to them with respect. He gave them his full attention, asked questions, and complimented them on their insights.

We would go into town on Saturday mornings, and I would listen to him speak to people that we passed. As we would walk away from the different conversations, he would always ask, "What did you learn?"

My father was not the only wise man who had opinions on listening. Here are a couple of examples:

"When you talk, you are only repeating what you already know. But if you listen, you may learn something new."
Dalai Lama

"Most of the successful people I've known are the ones who do more listening than talking."
Bernard Baruch

"The most basic of all human needs is the need to understand and be understood. The best way to understand people is to listen to them."
Ralph Nichols

"Being heard is so close to being loved that for the average person they are almost indistinguishable."
David Augsburger

Communicating with others is one of the keys to being successful, whether it be in school, with your career, or in relationships. You want to engage others, receive or pass along information, and when you do it well, you will hopefully leave the other person feeling good about spending time with you.

Communicating between the sexes is more difficult, but it is also a lot of fun. If you are trying to understand men . . . or women, it is important to understand that both sexes want the same thing, though they express it differently. We all want to be respected and understood.

Any relationships can grow and improve if you spend time getting to know the other person better. The best way to do that is by really listening to them. Hear what they have to say. Ask them questions about what is important to them. Listen to their story. You like to be heard, right? So do they.

We were created to be with others. We were created for community. You can spend a lifetime learning how to communicate with others; it will take a lifetime to do it well.

© 2019 Rob Corn, "Communicating with Men"

Anecdotes

The Facets of Man

Beautiful Soul, there are many categories about men that are sophisticated and complex, which can be summed up as men are often result-oriented.

Here are some highlights of the common traits of men from my experience:

Avoid Nagging

Nothing is more frustrating to a man than when his partner constantly asks him to do household chores, especially when he is watching sports or news; it sets him off. Also, a good percentage of men don't like doing chores because they are scared that they might do something wrong.

Fine Is Fine

If a man asks, "How are you?" and you say, "I'm fine," then he will act as if nothing is wrong. Men can't always identify emotions as quickly as women can. But having said that, don't ever think that men are completely insensitive.

Let Him Be

Sometimes a man wants to hang out with his male friends, and he will be happier if you join him with his friends. **A**

small dating tip: beer or another beverage may be his close friend, if you want to offer. (Wink.)

Give Him Space

Sometimes, he doesn't want to talk. You should be patient and not take it personally.

Men Are Not Multi-taskers

Unlike women, many men are single-minded and can do one thing at a time, so please don't expect to get a perfect result if you give him diverse DIY projects.

Men Are Competitive

Yes, that's right. Think of it this way. Why do you think he suddenly yells while watching cricket, football, or baseball? Or why do boxing matches have more of a male following? When in jobs, men like outperforming their peers.

Men Do Like to Commit

It's a common misconception that men don't like to commit. They do like to commit; it's just that it takes them a good amount of time to process.

Please Don't Ask, "Am I Fat?"

Especially for married couples, if you ask this question

every time you go out, then the conversation automatically goes into nagging mode. Frankly, many men don't really care if you are fat or not. What they care about the most about is whether you are happy or not.

Trust Him More

Trust the man in your life when he says he wants to be independent. He wants your love and support, but never in any way that tries to control or manipulate him. If you really want to give him advice, give him stats and facts. It might be more helpful.

On Opening Up

As a wife, girlfriend, or mother, if he looks stressed to you, ask him about it once. If he doesn't tell you what is bothering him, show him that you care for him. He will open up in a day or two, but never nag. If he still doesn't, it might be that he doesn't trust you enough or your waiting time could be longer. Don't make your doubt look too obvious.

Men Can Cook

Yes, men can cook and sometimes much better than their spouse. It's just that they only cook when they are happy and in a good mood or when it is essentially necessary.

Men Would Never Ask for Directions

Men are normally good drivers and are good at reading maps and directions, but rarely will they ever stop to ask directions, unlike women.

Men Prefer Intelligence

Intelligence and a sense of humor go together when a man is looking for a partner. They are normally good at judging whether your sense of humor is at-par with theirs or not, but they might never tell you that.

Men Love to Help Women

Almost every man would love to solve a woman's problems first, and then if he is willing, he might help a man in a similar situation.

Men's Hearts Are in Their Stomachs!

If you want to win a man's heart, prepare his favorite meal. Men always crave for good food.

Chit-chat Is Not Meant for Men

If you want to chit-chat or gossip, invite your female friends. Men are rarely interested or paying close attention to chit-chat. There's even a book titled, *Men Don't Listen* and *Women Can't Read Maps*, ha ha.

Man's Best Pal Is Dog

Have you ever observed why he spends more time alone with his dog? Besides, people who own dogs laugh more than those who have no pets—and men love to laugh.

Men Aren't Always Thinking about Sex

Yes, this is also a misconception that needs to be addressed. Men don't always care about looks and they are not always thinking about sex. It is quite natural that men are more likely to think about sex more often than women, but that doesn't mean that they have sex on their minds at all times. Speaking of looks, impress him with your wit, patience, understanding and caring nature.

Following these few tips on understanding a man doesn't guarantee you a sure-shot success, but still gives you a sneak peek into his mind.

© 2019 Rohit Sharma, "The Facets of Man"

Chapter Eighteen
Matters of the Heart

A Rose Shall Rise

All those tears you've cried are collected,
in a vase of flowers once neglected,
hidden in a heart and thus protected,
from your weakest moments disconnected.

And from your tears a rose shall rise above,
forged from the trials and tears, magnifying love!
It doesn't ill you; it just makes you stronger,
so wait a minute, won't be much longer!
Your rose shall rise singing unto the skies;
we shall wipe the tears from the crying eyes!
Your rose shall rise singing unto the skies,
uncaged thus, your heart shall fly to the skies!

A rose shall rise singing unto the skies;
take my hand and lift the veil from my eyes!
That rose shall rise singing unto the skies;
true beauty you shall see through open eyes!

© *25 September 2019 Whitney Rix Victory II, "A Rose Shall Rise"*

Behind the Thorns

The moments that we were laughing then,
before the candle reached the end,
love sighed quietly its desperation,
for we were fraught with fear's hesitation!
All too soon, the music shall end;
we must wait until we meet again.
The one last kiss, we shall always miss,
the one more minute of joy and bliss!

Suffer not this, a tragedy,
for it's a part of the plan you see.
Behind the thorns we find the beauty,
so please celebrate this time with me!
As love sighs quietly, its sweet despair,
hold so tightly the magic we share!
Behind the thorns we find the beauty,
so please celebrate this time with me!

And so, bottle up sweet memories,
and let their tales float upon the breeze,
to soon feed the roses yet to be.
Precious moments live on in stories,
and make a poetic history.

163

Moments tender and life's sweet glories,
behind the thorns we find the beauty;
always celebrate this time with me!

© 26 September 2019 Whitney Rix Victory II, "Behind the Thorns"

Reaching for the Stars and Beyond

As a father of five—eight, with our three children-in-law—I recently wrote the following as part of what I wished to impart to one of my children on marrying his sweetheart:

When particles in the universe are "entangled," they reflect and respond to each other—even across the universe. The connection is so deep that it seems to go against the known laws of nature. Albert Einstein could not believe that electrons across the universe could do this. There is a natural speed limit in the universe, which is the speed of light. The instantaneity of this reaction breaks the light barrier.

This can be what we call true love. However, humans are complex, and that complexity means that we are made of many particles and this is further complicated by the fluidity and nature of humans. It is highly problematic to get the majority of two persons in total sync—but that is what makes the game so interesting.

The universe is so very happy that you two found each other. We are stardust after all. The odds of all the "coincidences" required for our stardust to be where it is, in the time that it is, and with the connections it has found, have made it nothing less than monumental. Nobody in Las Vegas would bet on it.

The challenge that you two are meeting takes those odds to a new level and allows for your cosmic entanglement. May you continue to succeed at the game. It is all a game, albeit one with very serious universal consequences. But it requires constant work and attention to make the sync better and deeper and more fulfilling as the years go on.

I do speak from some experience. To be a father is a fortuitous blessing that is fortuitous in the coincidences required in becoming a husband and a blessing in the immeasurable rewards. However, it is the hardest job in the universe—second only to that of being a mother.

If you wish to dwell on it—and I am not advising you to do so—you may recall the ups and downs of growing up that led you to where you are today. You faced all those challenges and prepared yourself for the great place you are at today. I certainly recall them only as part of the package that has given me the most joy in my life. Your spouse and your children are, in my opinion, a major part of your foundation. They are the compound of your parents and those who came before you and your own achievements in setting up a life and home. We stand on the shoulders of those who came before us and your children will stand on your shoulders in their time.

Those brave souls who venture out into the cosmos to learn more about humanity's origins also provide for humanity's future. You and your chosen partner will now embark on a journey comparable to that of any astronaut. It requires confidence in yourself and your partner. It requires qualities and capabilities that you may not even realize you have. Teamwork will make the journey easier by far. Constant and ongoing learning will supplement your abilities to cope, overcome and go further than you can imagine.

You are reaching for the stars and perhaps even beyond. Buckle in for the ride and be confident as you countdown to your wedding day. This is not a cause for fear, but celebration. We look forward to continuing to watch you with pride and joy. You two have got the right stuff—so get to work.

Love you always.

© 2019 Milton H. Elbogen, "Reaching for the Stars and Beyond"

 # Anecdotes

Surviving Heartache

"There are wounds that never show on the body that are deeper and more hurtful than anything that bleeds."
Laurell K. Hamilton

The pain of losing someone close to us, especially our

biological parents, hurts the most and stays for a long time in our mind and heart before we get over the depression. If uncontrolled, it can lead to mental illness due to emotional stress for a long time. After losing a loved one to death or their leaving, we always feel like the world has just ended and we may see no reason to live anymore.

On the contrary, there is more knowledge to learn that brings happiness, love and compassion back to our lives—even after the great loss of our beloved parents or after a breakup.

Coping with such a great loss hasn't been and will never be easy.

"Mental pain is less dramatic than physical pain, but it is more common and also more hard to bear. The frequent attempt to conceal mental pain increases the burden: it is easier to say, 'My tooth is aching' than to say, 'My heart is broken.'"

C. S. Lewis

We can't avoid death or loss. They are processes we go through, and we have to face the task ahead of us.

What's the way forward after a loved one is gone? What will make you succeed? What about your future? Where do you see yourself heading? The best way is to first love yourself. Grieving about the dead won't bring them back to life.

Friends become our partners after the death of our beloved parents. In my growth, I came to realize that friends can have an even greater impact on us than our relatives. They supported me, gave me advice, comforted me and even connected me to other people. My happiness became their joy.

CHRISTINA GOEBEL & THE GOLDENHEARTS

We learn from friends and a real bond is built with them, making them part of our family. Get connected over social media and share your dreams and goals. This will help you to understand that people around the world are undergoing tougher moments than you are. You will be encouraged from their history too.

In February of 2003, I became depressed the day after my mother's burial. I was very lonely. People who came for the burial left. Everything changed suddenly. A week later, I became sick with a severe headache and stomach pain. I developed ulcers and couldn't eat. I didn't have an appetite and the memories of my best mum were only in my mind.

If the pain is complex and uncontrollable, seek advice from a psychologist, therapist, or other professional to help you get back to normal. However, it is not always an automatic process to forget the deceased or person you lost.

Orphans have little option but to work hard. Challenges we face build our character so that we can make this world a better place to be. A man with integrity will always be in a position to leave things better than the way he found it. Take good care of any position you are entrusted with as a responsibility. Do your best. It doesn't matter what type of job you do. For instance, I am a cleaner at a university in Nairobi, Kenya. I do whatever I signed to do on the contract for employment. I am responsible for my duty without any supervision. I keep my time as the days pass.

Always do whatever you can. You can't afford to be idle. As they say, "An idle mind is the devil's workshop." Ensure you gain financially at the end of the day.

"A life spent making mistakes is not only more honorable, but more useful than a life spent doing nothing."
George Bernard Shaw

Personally, I want to be on the list of the people who changed the world by making it a better place to be. I believe that my life is always in my hands, and that there is space for more lives. My dream is to come up with a foundation helping orphans and vulnerable families by restoring their hope and supporting them physically, socially and economically. I spend a lot of time with orphans in different orphanages, determining the challenges they face and supporting them since they are part of my life. Chase after your dream now. Stop postponing when to start. The time is now.

"Change will not come if we wait for some other person or some other time. We are the ones we've been waiting for. We are the change that we seek."
Barack Obama

"I believe that my life is always in my hands, and that there is space for more lives."
George Omondi Owiti

©2019 George Omondi Owiti, "Surviving Heartache"

With a Deeply Sad Heart, Since the Phone Is Silent . . . [or] Do You Remember Me?

Motto: *History cannot cheer you up, but let it be your true conscience. So, the story should be human: always full of humor and a bit of melancholy, just like the melancholy in the heroic music (not only of the Romantic era).*
The thought of historian Stanisław Herbst, extended by the author.

Dear Reader,

I'm thankful you wanted to come to these words! I have a positive attitude toward every person, including you. I have some social achievements, but I was probably lazier than you. Yes! I have managed to do some things, and I have also failed in many things. I'm just an ordinary person.

I have something important to tell you. We both know that every human has complete freedom. So, you can stop reading these words. You can jump to the mind of another author, or you can cry, thinking of your friend.

Do you feel lonely often, maybe not very often, but sometimes? Are you counting the minutes, waiting for someone you strongly think about to call you today?

Many times in my adult life, I counted on people to call me, but there were many weeks when none of them wrote me one text message. Not one!

You want to have a sincere conversation about life, often about important and long-lasting problems, and you want to talk about those ordinary troubles you have daily. "Maybe these little troubles will pass sooner after talking to my old friend," you may think? However, your phone is silent for weeks.

When the person you think about isn't calling or talking to you, he or she may often deeply think of you! They may have, for example, serious family misunderstandings, etc. Or maybe they have various problems. They don't want to admit their problems. That's why they don't contact you, Dear One!

Probably most of these people think of you as a human with a real, deep heart and you are important to them. They think many times that you are not calling them! They don't contact you, and you don't contact them, but they are in your thoughts and you are in theirs, sometimes in thoughts with heart that stay for a long, long time.

Dear, people call each other less from year to year, but music is always here for you when you are waiting and lonely. So, do you have favorite pieces of music and performances of them? How often do you turn on your close-to-the-heart music? Are you listening to favorite selections when you think about a friend or colleague? How many times last year did you call a friend (who hasn't called you for a long time) while listening to your warmest music?

It happened to me only about five-six times in the last five-six years. On my sad days, music gives me encouragement and vitality. Lately, I turn on my music and after a while, I call my friends!

I don't mean, Dear Reader, to play music that drowns out a telephone conversation. (Wink.) On difficult, sad days, when my smartphone is silent, I return to pieces of music that have vital energy and end victoriously. Have you searched to find your favorite winning music, such as the "Toccata D BWV 912" by J.S. Bach?

I was surprised that this piece of music that I know from my youth has been recorded by many artists around the world. This isn't a musical hit—and yet, people everywhere play it. Here are different interpretations of the toccata. View these videos and look for more. Can you hear many (any) differences between them?

https://www.youtube.com/watch?v=hOARPGN_A-A from 4:28 by Céline Frisch
https://www.youtube.com/watch?v=DkKeZN7kxKo from 4:47 by Robert Hill (another version of the toccata)
https://www.youtube.com/watch?v=eJwHnM979YA from 7:08 by Sara Johnson Huidobro
https://www.youtube.com/watch?v=pKm44pJkIAo from 5:19 by Chiara Massini
https://www.youtube.com/watch?v=zxNOdXzo-a4 from 6:58 by Anthony Newman
https://www.youtube.com/watch?v=p8XuCRTZxdw from 1:15 by Yves Rechsteiner
https://www.youtube.com/watch?v=OHHt87Bnyxo by Scott Ross
https://www.youtube.com/watch?v=cK4mkP0KbjU by Andreas Staier

To compare the performance of the last part of this toccata (up to the end of this piece), I give you the minute and the second in the video. Keep in mind that the toccata by J. S. Bach is intended primarily for the harpsichord. Of course, you can find other performances that will be closer to your heart or personality.

When you think about your friend and you miss her or him, look for music of your choice. Does this make goodly sense, Dear Reader? Then you will have something to share that you both may enjoy. Perhaps they will share something with you like I did just now.

I thought about one more idea for when I miss a friend. I can write a text message or e-mail to someone (who has not called me for a long time) with the following words: "I think of you often! I think of you in my heart three-five times a week." I can add a question: "Do you ever think about me when we're not on the phone?" I could continue, "For months, I wanted to call you several times, but did not dare; I don't understand why." I can add: "And do you have favorite types of music and what are your favorite performances?"

You will come closer to her or his heart with music.

Not everyone will answer you (you know this, don't you?), but if you are consistent and believe more and more, the day will come that you will gain a real friend for life and maybe music will connect you like instruments in a symphony!

Your closest friend will be smarter than any performer of any music. Yes, your friend will understand *you*! You, the boy or girl, or the woman or man with a real heart for people who is smart, beautiful and deep. You will be a great person for them!

I do believe you will succeed within a few months, my cordial, beloved Golden Heart! Let music fill your heart!

* * *

P.S. Here is my gift for you, Dear Reader: F. Chopin's "Mazurka C Op. 67 No. 3," and I searched everywhere available to record it especially for you! https://www.youtube.com/watch?v=1IuH4m8sggY

© 2019 Michał Domaszewicz, "With a Deeply Sad Heart, Since the Phone Is Silent . . . [or] Do You Remember Me?"

Two of Michał's closest friends left this world long before the COVID-19 times. He is a professional musician (not an artist), an experienced music historian of 18th-19th century music, and a former student of the greatest Polish expert of 19th century music, the world-renowned Chopinologist, Professor Zofia Chechlińska. He is also a team sports hobbyist, though he has too little knowledge of baseball! (Wink.)

Chapter Nineteen
How to Do the Right Thing

Your Footprint Leaves an Impact for All

Beautiful Soul, from the day you were born, you made decisions whether you wanted to or not. It's part of life and learning, and it becomes more difficult as you get older. What will change is the challenge that a decision brings, and a clear understanding of doing what will better your life and that of those around you. It all begins with something that you were born with and that everything bears inside.

Love. It comes from within, and it is your answer to everything the world will throw at you. Love is the right answer, the right thing, and the most important gift and guide you are given. It is what each of us has in common, and why we are all one because of this incredible energy that resides deep within our soul. Everything in this universe is created with it, and each of us are brought into this world with nothing but that love which saturates our hearts. It is up to us to find this love, listen to our hearts before our minds, and understand that by following this love, we will consistently make better choices and decisions.

We have something within us called a gut feeling. This is a feeling inside that warns us when something isn't right; it gives us a chance to rethink our decisions before we act on them. This feeling from deep within our soul automatically sends a signal from our heart as a quick reminder that it comes first. It's like an alarm that sounds, a sign from above, a chance to stop time and analyze what direction we should take, and what will be in our best interest. But what is it, and why do we get it?

Perhaps you felt it when you were younger. Your friends were teasing someone, and you thought that you had to join in so they would like you. But before you made the decision to join in on teasing that person, you felt that gut feeling. Just for a moment, that feeling deep inside warned you it wasn't right, that it would hurt that person's feelings, and that you shouldn't do it. That feeling made you realize that you could change that person's life forever, and if it were you who was being teased, how would it make you feel?

As we grow older, our decisions and choices become much harder and more complicated, but you will get better at making the right choice if you take your time and lead your decision making with your heart. You are going to hurt others, loved ones, and close friends, not because you want to, but because there is just no other way. This is part of life, and everyone will heal and grow from the experience. We must put our best interest first in our choices, not for greed or because of arrogance, but for our happiness and contentment for the journey ahead. Putting our interests first is something that most of us have trouble with because we don't want to hurt others in the process.

You will make many bad decisions in your lifetime; it's inevitable. I don't believe there is a single soul on this Earth that hasn't made at least one bad decision. So really look back at one when you make it, not in a bad way to dwell on it, but to understand where you went wrong and what led you to make your final decision. These choices will stand out and educate you. They will replay when you have similar decisions in the future, and they may hurt more than you can imagine. But everyone goes through this, and everyone learns the same way.

If your gut feeling speaks to you, listen closely; it's for a reason. It is your best defence to avoid a choice you may regret in the future. If your choices are for everyone else and you are not happy in your life, then you need to rethink them. If you are not happy in life, you pass this on to everyone around you and it results in a ripple effect. We can only try to do the right thing, and I believe if we lead with love, we are doing the best that we can.

I have made many wrong decisions along my journey, but these decisions have taught me valuable lessons. I wish someone had taught me long ago about the importance of following my heart and putting more trust into the love that fills it. Until I learned to truly love myself and others, I had no direction, no core. There was a dim light that flickered from within, and I just existed. My decisions were based on sadness, despair, loneliness, anxiety, and anger—making it easy to ignore my gut feeling.

The best and most life-changing decision I have made in my life is to put my heart first and my brain second. My inner well-being, my environment, and my entire life has flourished more than I could ever imagine. I love myself; I love others, and my journey is a better one. Sure, I still make decisions that are not the best, but I have learned from them, and I know deep inside that I did the best I could when I made them. If I try to base my decisions on the knowledge that what I project comes back to me, my decisions will reflect the kindness and light that shines inside my heart, benefiting myself and others.

Remember, we ARE given choices. There really are no excuses if you ignore all your morals and gut feelings and guide your decision with anger or pure spite. When you are pressured, angry, or in a negative place, these are huge warning signs that the decision you are about to make will be the wrong one. Do everything in your power to Pause, Breathe, Think, and Act. Pause. Take a deep breath. Think about the choice you are about to make and if it came from your heart. Is it in your best interest? Will it hurt others? What are the consequences? And finally, make your decision and act on it. Always keep in mind that this choice and your actions are going to pave the path to your future.

So, what is the right thing? Is there a right thing? Honestly, I am not sure. But I have learned that if I take my time making my choice, analyze my decision before I act, listen to my gut, and always lead with my heart and soul, I have done the best that I can. It's all any of us can do. Much love to you, Beautiful Soul. Always follow your heart.

© 2019 Todd Sarsons (Budokaizen), "Your Footprint Leaves an Impact for All"

Chapter Twenty
Don't Give Up on Your Dreams

Dare to Dream

My name is Jason. I'm just a very average snooker player with a background in theatre who decided to create an event that I would buy tickets to myself.

Back in the 1970s, a lot of families were poor. It didn't make them unhappy, but it meant they had to make choices and budget for essentials in a way many people don't now. For me, we could only watch the television if we had two shillings (ten pence) to put in the meter on the back. For my mum and dad, it was a way of ensuring that when the rental had to be paid on the TV, the money was there. It did however mean that sometimes my snooker coverage went off air, and my screen was replaced with darkness. I dreamed of a day when that would not be the case.

I'd watch snooker with my grandfather, a navy veteran of the Russian convoys. Despite the limitations of money, I saw enough to learn the nicknames and study the styles of the top boys: Hurricane, Whirlwind, and Grinder. I was mesmerized by their flamboyance, their champagne lifestyles and their fame. I badgered Grandpa to take me to the snooker hall and eventually I owned my own cue—an E.J. Riley, Joe Davis one piece, in ash; it was a beauty. It was a dream.

Childhood memories are scarce but my first visit to play a game of snooker on a full-size table with Grandpa Hocking is vivid. After my mates' six-foot by three, it felt like a football field. I wasn't even sure I could hit the ball that far, but I was hooked. From thirteen to sixteen, that place was a second home to me and my friends. The daily routine was to get in from school, make a quick change, head out the door with a "Bye, Mum," and then rush off to the Men's Institute. I'd only return when darkness descended, or when we'd run out of blagging one of the older boy's money for the table light. I was living the dream.

The cherished moments of our time together in that snooker room left a lasting impression on me; no doubt the tobacco cloud probably did too. Happy times and lifelong friendships were all based around a twelve-foot by six-foot piece of furniture. I was still dreaming.

By the time I left home at eighteen, I'd already secured the County Under-21 Snooker title, but I wasn't leaving home to play snooker. I wanted to be an actor.

I wanted a better life than my parents had. It hurt me seeing them struggle to try and not let me or my brother go without. I made a promise that it wouldn't just be at Christmas time that I would get to drink pop.

In 1998, both my parents died. I was just twenty-eight and felt alone, vulnerable. I channelled my grief and anger into determination and drive, not always getting it right—in fact, getting it wrong on many occasions, but I learnt and listened and refused to give up. I was still dreaming.

In 2001, frustrated at not getting any acting roles, I wrote a play about 1960s playwright Joe Orton and cast myself in the main role. It ran in London for four weeks and lost me thousands, and the Times described my acting as "ordinary." I was maybe deluded, but I was still dreaming.

I had years of debt, too many early mornings delivering newspapers and too many late nights serving pizzas. I walked home in the cold because I couldn't afford a bus and grew my hair long because I couldn't afford to have it cut.

There was no silver spoon, no helping hand, but there was determination to get up every time I was knocked down. I refused to give up on my dream.

I never thought that an idea to stage a 2010 snooker exhibition with my hero, Alex Higgins, would within three years grow into an event that was watched by more than twelve million on Eurosport.

I never thought I'd be able to one day call Ronnie O'Sullivan and Jimmy White my good friends.

I never knew where this crazy idea would take me.

I just dared to dream . . . and never gave up. Don't let the present dictate your future.

© *2019 Jason Francis, "Dare to Dream"*

Anecdotes

A Whisper from Within

Dear Beautiful Soul, every person on Earth is created with love, for a purpose, and in a special way specifically for that purpose. Everything about you makes you different from the rest of us and gives you your own identity. You are meant to be your own individual and have different ideas, different goals, and passions. Your life dreams are all these things wrapped up in a thought, a feeling, and plan suited especially for you to give you a life of happiness and contentment—your blueprint and guide to build a lifetime of bliss.

But many of us don't pay attention to our dreams. We are scared to fulfill them or are driven away by the input of others. Many of us think that we are incapable of reaching these goals and dreams. We don't believe in ourselves. The biggest mistake we can make is to ignore these dreams. They are created just for us. They have all been planned out with love and our best interests in mind. They're our destiny, and we need to pay attention to them.

Think of your dreams as the best gifts you could receive, something that will complete your life and give you endless joy. They're yours and only yours, and nobody can take them from you. Your dreams represent everything that completes your soul, fascinates you, excites you, brings the passion out in you, and restores the joy in your life. Each dream that replays throughout your life and calls out to get your attention has a purpose and reason.

It's important that we chase each dream that we have. We need to do this in order to understand if it the one for us. It's that one dream that we will spend most of our lives searching for, and that dream will complete us. But how will we know when we have found it?

You will know because it will be the dream that stands out amongst all that you will have throughout your life. This dream will never stop replaying in your mind and it will continuously whisper to your soul. You will know.

You will chase many dreams in your life. Every dream that you chase brings understanding, direction, and strength. You build courage; face your fears and grow. Each dream teaches you things that you need to experience to mold you into the best person you can be. They are building blocks for your soul. They will come and go, and some will take you many years to chase and fulfill. Some will even take a lifetime.

You will encounter everything you could ever imagine chasing your dreams: happiness, sadness, despair, love, adventure, and the list goes on. Every dream will give you direction and show you why it may not be the perfect mix for giving you the happiness for the rest of your life that you thought it would. This is part of your life, and it's a natural process that each of us will go through. Dream building is fine tuning your destiny.

One of the biggest hurdles you will face chasing your dreams is fear. It will put false doubt in your mind and make you believe things that just aren't true. Doubt makes you believe that your goals are out of reach, that you don't deserve them, or that they can never happen because they seem so surreal. But how can you believe what fear is telling you if you never face it head on and prove it untrue? Fear is one of the hardest things that life will ever throw at you, and it is the most difficult thing in life to overcome. It will show itself in many forms, appear every chance it can, and always stay right beside you if you let it. Fear is created for a reason, and when you defeat it, it opens an entirely new world. It builds great strength and confidence, changes your outlook on things, and is another part of your creation that helps you become the best person you can be in your journey.

Your dreams are yours, and only yours, and it's important that you remember that. Nobody can take them from you. Another obstacle you may face is other people trying to steer you away from your destiny, but this too is part of life, and it teaches you and helps you grow. Some may be jealous or feel scared that if you fulfill your dream you will change, that they will never see you again, or that it's not for you. You may have to let go of a loved one. You may even lose friends, but it is for your best interest; understand that it is part of the plan designed specifically for you. It's difficult to face, but when it is over, you will find out that it has a purpose, and that it has taught you many things that will help make you a stronger, better person, and that it will make the rest of your life better. Be kind to everyone. Don't judge them for their actions, and understand that everyone that comes into your life, comes into it for a reason. Love them for who they are, regardless of the circumstance. Everyone involved will grow from the experience and move on; it's the way of life.

So, this one dream that cries out to you every second of your life, the one that is all you can think of, that brings sheer excitement and joy when you think about it, this is your destiny. It is your bliss and will pave the way to your future. Let nothing stand in your way to fulfill it and make it yours, nothing. You're the only obstacle, nothing else. Whatever you believe, then that is exactly what will play out for you. If you don't believe that your dream can come true, it won't. It's up to you to believe, have patience and understanding, and realize that if you want something badly enough, there is nothing that can hold you back.

Life is but a dream, my friends. Reach out and chase them all. These dreams are everything that makes you happy wrapped up in the most beautiful gift you could ever ask for and they are made just for you. Don't give up on your dreams. Begin each day visualizing what it will be like to be living in that dream, and all that you did to be there—your triumphs, sacrifices, determination, and the strength you gained, as well as the courage it took. Replay it and do everything you can to remind yourself of it every chance you can. Every part of a dream is the most beautiful thing you will encounter—the dream, the chase, and the fulfillment.

Never stop chasing your dreams. Never.

Much love to you, Dear Soul. May all your dreams come true.

© 2019 Todd Sarsons (Budokaizen), "A Whisper from Within"

God's Children

Hello, friends! Let's remember that we're all God's children, each one of us. Humans are a one big family of Earthlings. It's because of the prevailing system that most have been assigned guardians or parents. A few unfortunate ones have had their parents snatched away from them.

Let's remember, we were all blessed with faculties to help sustain us to thrive on our own, given the right attitude. Then there's nature to nurture to take care of us.

I've seen numerous instances where kids have been ruined through faulty parenting. Take the case of one of my school mates—a topper, genius, and a potential electronics wizard. While we were still struggling with the basic principles of electricity, my schoolmate was inventing electronic gadgets. Alas, his dad forced him into the family business. A few years later, we got reports of my schoolmate having gone ashtray. A genius ended up as a drug addict.

Take the case of a friend, a happy fun-loving guy who hid a deep, inner pain. His dad, an army officer, was a strict disciplinarian who insisted on blind obedience. My friend avoided discussing his dad, but when he did, he referred to him as Colonel So-and-So. As soon as he got a job, he went off on his own and never went back home. He made a life for himself that he was craving.

Then there are countless seemingly successful people who became what their dads wanted them to become. I've spoken to quite a few of them. While they seem normal, happy, well off, and successful family men, deep down there's emptiness, regret, and a deep feeling of discontent.

My dear friends, you're not as unfortunate as you think. You're free to do your own thing. Your circumstances are just different from others' situations. Build up a positive self-esteem and keep smiling. No matter what, be positive. In the place of a family, you'll have friends who will provide all the loving care and warmth you need. Just learn to recognize the real friends from mere hangers on for advice and guidance! You have a built-in friend, guide, and mentor: your conscience. Follow it and you'll never go wrong. Hold your head high and stay on the move.

Two things you must guard against are desolation and depression. Talk to your inner self daily and you'll never be lonely. Keep giving yourself pep talks. Loneliness is a state of mind. There are so many people who are lonely, even when surrounded by caring people. Periodic contact with nature will give you a feeling of belonging. Never give in to hopelessness. Whenever you feel down, go into the wilderness to some beautiful spot and you'll experience an overwhelming feeling of wellbeing. Inculcate love for good books and healthy habits. Give out love, kindness, and consideration to get it back manifold.

Through daily introspection, you'll get to know your talents and aptitude—and activities that set your soul on fire with passion! Pursue them relentlessly, with grit and determination. Fight negativity from the word go.

Remember, you're all God's children; nothing can hold you back. You're special. Go all out and make your dreams come true, because if you allow yourself to do that, nothing can hold you back.

© 2019 Pratosh Vashi, "God's Children"

Chapter Twenty-One
Playing Sports and Being Fit

My father played almost all sports and games and coached soccer. He played football and ran track in high school, and was accomplished in baseball, basketball, tennis, volleyball, frisbee and any other sport he attempted. While running came naturally to me, Dad taught me many skills pertaining to sports and fitness. My first lesson was the benchmark of many coaches I have met: hard work pays off.

Practice Pays Off

When the girls at school said they wanted to tryout for softball, it sounded fun. I had hit a ball at school. One day of tryouts proved to me that I couldn't catch well. To begin with, I had a brand-new glove that was so stiff that I could barely open it or catch balls (practice makes the gloves softer and easier to use).

They threw ground balls to us and I didn't know how to use the glove to catch a ball coming at me. The balls came and went, leaving me staring at the ground and my empty glove. They threw pop flies, which I caught reasonably well. Then, they batted balls to us in the outfield. My amateur performance landed me the not-so-coveted position of left fielder. My father saw it as a challenge for us to improve my position on the team by working hard. Looking back at it, baseball and softball teams must have those fielders, so just because they are farther away from some game play doesn't mean they aren't important. They are.

Dad knew I had more ability than I had displayed (that would be true of all of us), but it boiled down to my needing practice at catching and throwing balls. He took me into the back yard, and we practiced throwing and catching. He showed me the various ways to catch balls and how to position my hand and arm to throw a ball for a longer distance. Later, we went to the softball field where I would play, and we practiced throwing and catching there to familiarize me with the area. He batted balls for me to catch. I learned to run quickly to be where I anticipated a fly ball would land. We spent days practicing and he worked me until I was tired every time. When I was ready to quit, he always asked for a little more.

Batting with a team also differed from the way we did it in physical education class. I had to bat several times in a softball game, making it less frequent for me to naturally hit balls and run bases. Dad took me to batting cages where balls were mechanically thrown to me. He also practiced with me in fields where I had enough space to hit balls hard. If I had batted in my backyard, I would have had to hold back to avoid hitting neighbors' windows. You need a place where you can let it loose with full power. Watching for where I made mistakes, Dad suggested how to improve my batting technique. What came naturally no longer mattered. How I could perform better was his focus.

It was the same when Dad coached me in track. Running fast was not enough. Setting records was a temporary joy. After a race, the hard work began, trying to see what held me back. He would have me run the race distance ten times in a row to build endurance. He studied how I ran, the position of my legs and toes, how I breathed during running. We explored new ways for me to push out of the starting blocks faster. We focused on warm-ups so I didn't get injuries and on not eating or drinking a few hours before races because sprinters can't usually keep down food and drinks when they run full speed. There was even a bit of track applied to my softball practices. I learned how to run full speed across the bases and then tag my foot quickly on the base. I learned how to lead away from a base to steal a base (run to the next base while the pitcher wasn't looking). Then I had to work combinations running to catch a ball hit by my opponent, hustling and throwing it to the pitcher, baseman, or catcher to strike them out before they could reach the base.

Though it seemed sudden to my coach and teammates that I improved dramatically as a ball player and track and field athlete, the reason I made the all-star softball team (the teams where the league's best players were nominated by coaches to participate) and track championships was because I worked harder than some of my peers. That is all. During the same period, any players who didn't practice outside of our team's games would not improve much during a season, while those of us who placed more priority on the sports ended up on special teams.

Good Sportmanship

My second lesson was in sportsmanship. One day, my softball teammates were upset because we lost. In the beginning, we were a lousy team with not much experience. We finished the game and there wasn't much excitement in congratulating the members of the other team, a softball and baseball tradition.

Dad saw our grumpy faces and growling about losing and immediately called my attention to it. He said that good sportsmanship was as important as being a good player. The other team worked harder than us most likely, and that is why they won. We should thank them for the opportunity to play and try harder next time by practicing more before the game. Because they had played so well, we would have to improve our skills and that was a great thing. I got a lot of enjoyment out of congratulating other teams after that talk with my father and have since viewed my competitors as temporary opponents, but also as people who love my sport too. Good sportsmanship allows us to enjoy our sport fully. Oh, we still want to win on the field—just to do it gracefully.

Believe in Those Who Believe in You

When I participated in track and field, Dad pushed me harder because I was a natural sprinter. I loved it from day one. The kids had chased me at recess, and I ran fast enough to escape, which let me know I had some ability. However, I only wanted to run as far as I could easily do—and that was a short distance. My father suggested that I run a farther distance that was not natural to me and I didn't accept that easily. It was not uncommon for us to disagree passionately about what I could or could not do. One of my regrets is that I resisted my father and coach so much when he believed that I could do more. If you think about it, that's a compliment. You want people to believe you CAN. If they believe you can do better, keep your complaining mouth shut and try it and see. Maybe they are right! (Wink.)

My father and track coaches pushed me to practice more often and increase my speeds by drills and practice runs, to strengthen my muscles by working out on weight equipment in the gym, and to run a little farther than felt easy. My speed increased as well as my stamina, and I went from running the shortest sprint to a longer one, and from running sprints only to adding on the long jump and shotput field events. They encouraged me to try other events, such as the high jump and hurdles, and neither felt comfortable—but at least I attempted them to see.

As an adult, challenging myself was an important part of my sports training from Dad and so many male and female coaches. When I saw the pull-up bar in the all-female gym, I tried to pull myself up and couldn't. This didn't make sense to me, since I could lift a good amount of weight and used several weight machines daily to increase my strength. In fact, I didn't see any women attempting pull ups at my gym. Athletes seek a coach when they need expertise, so I asked a trainer at the gym if she knew how I could do the pull ups. She said she couldn't do them either. Without a coach, I was left with something all my coaches had taught me. There is a way.

There Is a Way

My arm muscles didn't seem strong enough to lift me as far as this high pull-up bar. But what if I lowered myself first? Could I lift myself if I had gained momentum? I put a firm chair below the pull-up bar so that I stood even with it and lowered my body down from the pull-up position and then lifted myself back up to the bar. I did one pull up! I wasn't impressed with that much, because I could do only one that day. However, I knew that with training, patience, and perseverance, I could eventually do two pull ups and more. I set a goal for myself of completing ten—one day. Because this was a major challenge, my short-term goal was to do one more each day. If you are a young man or adult male, then you may wonder why doing pulls ups was a problem for me at all, so here is another lesson: male and female anatomy differs greatly. While women may not compete well with you in upper body strength in the gym, they may very well challenge you in leg strength, so we each have our strengths.

Every day that I went to the gym, I stretched and did a round of weights, jogging, rowing and other aerobic activities, and attempted more pull ups. Some days, I did one more than the day before. Other days, it was difficult to do any. Out of all the activities in the gym, pull up were the most difficult for me and would guess for most of the other women. Over a period of weeks, I increased the number I could do. The next time that I saw the trainer, I had just completed thirteen pulls ups. She said that she was going to work up to doing the same. Other women had watched me, and I knew they wondered if they could do the same. With practice and patience, they can.

You Can Do More than You Think You Can

Dearheart, you can do things beyond your current ability. Increasing your athletic ability is continually asking more of yourself—not a lot, but a little each day. If you jog for five minutes, maybe the next day, you can try for five minutes and fifteen seconds. If you can lift only so much weight today, try five pounds more tomorrow. If you can only lift something eight times today, try for nine the next day.

While it inspiring to see athletes do things that seem beyond human strength, remember that one day long ago, they felt that they could do no better—and then determined to try harder anyway. Many people have astounding physical ability and you may be one of them. As for the champions, those are the ones who dedicate daily, weekly, and monthly practice and push themselves to do more than before.

Your greatest competition is yesterday's progress. The goal is simple —beat what you did yesterday. Athletes consult coaches and other athletes regarding safe practices and ways to improve their skills. They take care of their bodies so that injuries don't hold them back. A little cautious progress is way better than a lot of reckless attempts at improvement that hurt your body and put you behind your previous efforts to recuperate.

Proper Preparation

I taught a stellar athlete who was a basketball star for the school. One day, he fell on the ground, grasping his leg. I sent a student to get the coach. The coach asked if the student had drunk enough water that day, to which the student said no. The coach told me that those cramps came on with dehydration.

Other athletes don't stretch before competing and sometimes incur serious muscle injuries or pain. As with any activity, the proper preparation and care is needed to perform at your best and repeat that process. The coach had warned the players to drink enough water daily and if they didn't listen —they would suffer later. While that player hurt his leg muscle, he could have as easily gotten cramps during a game from dehydration.

My coaches ingrained in me to warm up with stretches before running, lifting weights, or doing activities that might stress my body. I don't prefer stretching at the gym. I do that at home or in the locker room because I feel more comfortable. If I forget, then I will do that after exercise. It is still beneficial for those days you forget to do that before exercising. At the competitive level, warming up the muscles is essential, and you can do great damage to your body when you use 100 percent of your strength. I have seen some coaches not enforce warming up before high-level competition and would not omit that. A few coaches would sacrifice your health for their goals. Your body is a beautiful machine. Care for it well. Select coaches who show you how and say no to those whose practices do harm. You need your body for life.

Try several sports and if any interest you, locate the best teachers and learn ways to increase your skill, strength, and endurance. This is how to know if sports or fitness is one of your gifts! Dad considered sports integral to a teen's happiness when their hormones give them bad moods. Making yourself tired from exercise gets you out of a bad mood at any age! (Smile.) Because eating healthily and exercising brings people great satisfaction and improved health, this is one of the greatest secrets for a healthier, stronger, happier life.

Chapter Twenty-Two

How Not to Get in Your Own Way

You are beautiful. You were born in beauty. In beauty, your life can grow and blossom to bless the world and those you love—and beyond. You were meant to be a blessing to the wide world that enfolds and embraces us all. As you've been blessed with life, so your life can bless others. Yet, you sense there is something wrong. Since you've grown in understanding and in maturity, you've begun to feel that you have something to offer, something special and unique to yourself: perceptions, insights, skills and even love—but you can't release those things. They never see the light of day. Maybe you're mistaken; maybe you don't possess those qualities. But you know you do! You can feel the frustration of not being your best and gifting the world with yourself.

Perhaps somebody is blocking you or doesn't want you to succeed. Maybe you have enemies that are working against you or the world is just a bad place that is against you. Or possibly you have all the rotten, bad luck!

You've grown and experienced enough that you know none of that is true—none of it! But, you're confused. What is going on? Why can't I release the best of myself!

The first step in your quest to be your best and get out of your own way is to really know yourself. Grapple with your deepest thoughts and your most powerful emotions. Become aware of your reactions to others and to yourself—at the deepest level, not only to what seems apparent on the surface.

Almost always when you truly explore your inner being, you will take notice of something that has been happening perhaps for a very long time. A voice has been speaking to you from inside your consciousness, and that that voice has been relentlessly negative.

When that voice speaks—the voice that tells you shouldn't do it because you can't do it, because you're not good enough, and you never will be able to do it, because you never were good enough—find time for a moment or two when you experience the feeling without judging or fighting it, or getting mad at yourself. Just watch that feeling. Don't resist it. You need calmness now to access the better, truer parts of your nature. One of the most important parts of that nature is compassion.

Compassion, and through compassion, love is at the core of every healthy human being. When you speak with caring and love to a parent, friend, or anyone you deeply care about, you are expressing your appreciation of their uniqueness, and your support for them as a human being. You could never do any less for them, and you would gladly do more. I believe you are, at your deepest level, a person of compassion. But, if you're honest with yourself, you know you've talked to yourself pretty harshly: you can't do it; you aren't good enough; even—you're worthless.

These are words you would never utter to anyone, let alone someone you care about, yet you talk to yourself that way—and often!

When that happens, take the compassion that you show others, and every time that harsh voice speaks, counter it with the gentleness that is at your core. Make that voice the trigger for the kindness that has always been yours. Now that voice, which is a part of you, and that you'll now begin to love, can be greeted with your innate compassion—every time. You'll be so different, and that change will play out in the world, because you're getting out of your own way!

But there are other pitfalls. This is one of the most common: the idea of perfection. Who doesn't want to be perfect? You hear it all the time: she wants the perfect job, the perfect house in the suburbs, the perfect marriage (with 2.5 kids). Who wouldn't? Who wouldn't want their work, writing, art, relationships, and life to be flawless?

In wishing for perfection, you're setting up a goal that is so immense, overwhelming, and unattainable that the only thing you set up is yourself—for failure! If you set your goal for something so high that it can't be reached, then every time you take the field, pick up your guitar, speak to a group, draw a picture, or simply interact with others, you burden yourself with expectations and harsh demands that will drain you and eventually crush you.

Here is a quote from the great concert cellist, Yo Yo Ma that sums it up beautifully for me, and I hope for you: "I welcome that first mistake! . . . Then I can get on with the performance and turn off the part of the mind that judges everything. And it's when . . . I'm lost in the emotion of that music that I'm performing at my best."

Get lost in life with all its messiness and imperfection, and you'll free yourself from self-imposed pressures to meet a deadening, sterile, perfectionist standard. You'll free yourself to do what you were born to do, which is to be your truest self. That is the self that the universe is ready to embrace and love!

Sometimes, when you've come to grips with the things we've just talked about, you might still find yourself doing something that will hold you back. Perhaps you've freed yourself from negative self-talk or you've left the sallow ghost of perfection behind, but you're still counting, tallying, and comparing yourself to others. She has this, and I don't. He has that, and I don't. Or, she is so much further ahead than I am; he is moving so much faster than I am; why can't I progress like she does?

Let those thoughts be triggers for the knowledge that you are a unique person who has a unique pace of self-discovery, progress, and achievement. Only your pace is right for you. If you're doing your best and working at improving yourself and your work; if you're deepening your relationships with your loved ones, and you walk in compassion with everyone you meet, then you're doing everything you can. Now, you can let go. Now, you can let it happen for you. You won't be in your way anymore.

Even though I may never meet you, I love you. And all along, the universe has been trying to love you. Now you can love it back. Throw open your arms and let it in—it loves you.

© *2019 Kent Burles, "How Not to Get in Your Own Way"*

Chapter Twenty-Three
Coping with Loss

Coping with Loss

My parents died during my early childhood stage after a long struggle with HIV/AIDS infection. I lost my dad when I was eight months old in early 1997. My mum died in 2003. This caused me to be raised in an orphanage due to my vulnerable state.

People often quickly forget the dead, but when it comes to parents or dear ones, the memories are always alive. They are unforgettable. Sixteen years after my mother's death, I remember her as if she's still here. I imagine how smiling and lovely she was, how she sang sweet songs to put me to sleep, how she worked hard at the farm to get me food to eat. That love is still active but in a passive way. My mother's love and memory are irreplaceable.

I am always thinking about how my life would have been if my parents were still around. Prayers, reading inspiring words, listening to favorite songs, talking with friends and working hard comfort me to accept my situation. The only thing left is "BUT." But they are deceased.

The day my mother's burial took place, loneliness was the order of the day. Things were not making sense at all. The days were very dull. Time was not moving, and everything was boring.

I struggled for a long time before understanding who I am and accepting that. I lost the respect of people around me. I wasn't feeling any love. I couldn't think of anything good but always had negative thoughts. It took me two to three months to make friends with a desk mate in school.

I was treated cruelly in hardship, without love, and this made me an introvert until now. I had very low self-esteem and no courage. The only thing left was to die.

One day in 2010, missionaries came to the orphanage to share with us the good news they had. The story of each of the orphans was revealed when we sat down at the hall. Two of my friends' stories were much more painful. First, a sister orphan was dumped on the railway line covered with rugs when she was just two days old. She was picked up two minutes before the train could run over her.

Secondly, a brother orphan was saved from a sewage septic tank when he was thrown inside to die. But grace was sufficient for them, since they were rescued and now, they are in college.

We grew up together at the orphanage. We were taught and well-taken care of there. Each of us was given a pen pal and this made me gain hope and confirm that there are people with golden hearts who have an open heart to comfort and show love to orphans. My mindset changed. The world turned out to be beautiful. I met friends and at long last, I accepted who I really was.

Yes, I had no parents, but it's beyond my capacity. It's uncontrollable. I had to be concerned about my future. I had to let go of every setback. I started working hard at my studies and my grades changed.

"Observe your cat. It is difficult to surprise him. Why? Naturally his superior hearing is part of the answer, but not all of it. . . He's not thinking about his job or his image or his income tax. He is putting first things first, principally his physical security. Do likewise."
Jeff Cooper

In 2007, we had post-election violence and I was forced to return to my uncle's at the village for safety. Being an adult orphan is one of the hardest life transitions a person can experience.

I was sensitive enough. I could clearly tell from the looks of things that I wasn't welcomed fully at the village. It was like I added more burdens to my uncle. I knew there was no love, but that was the only place I could stay. One day, I failed to graze the cattle on time, so my aunt got angry and said, "I did not tell widows to die for me to struggle taking care of their children." I felt much pain and the memories of my parents came alive again. I was lonely, so I visited my parents' grave to mourn and say how I really missed them and wished they were alive.

My education became stressful and complicated. Because I was good in class, I believed that education was the only hope to brighten my outlook. I registered at a local school for my seventh grade at the age of twelve. I worked at a farm to raise my fees. I could miss a class for a week every month to raise the fee and still emerge to be among top three after examinations.

Working for seven hours a day on the farm paid me little, so I rarely used to eat. I could only afford to take tea or sometimes porridge every night to manage my condition for three years.

High school was more expensive, and I couldn't pay for it. So, I thought of going back at the orphanage to be enrolled for the ninth grade. For the first time, I was rejected but allowed to spend a night with other kids. My peers joined high school and it pained me so much that I couldn't make it myself. So, I thought of waking up at four o'clock every morning to wash the van and the car for the director of the orphanage to win her trust to allow me back at school. I washed the car and the van for a month, and this created a way for me to be accepted and allowed to join high school.

High school was still owned by the director, so I didn't wait for the new uniforms and shoes. I just asked for exercise books. I took old shoes from a pit and took it to a cobbler to repair it since I didn't have any tools to do that. I joined the school without a full school uniform but a week later, I got new uniforms from the director.

Since it was a boarding school at the orphanage, we cooked for ourselves and I felt it was better than how I struggled before. At least food was provided, and I wasn't sleeping hungry. I wasn't lonely compared to the village.

Though I had many struggles after the loss of my parents, I am continuing college.

Despite my loss, I taught myself to learn much more from animals and birds, because I felt animals behave better than some human beings. For instance, a hen never gets tired of laying eggs. Determined, she lies on them for twenty-one days. With patience, she reduces her eating habits to lose weight and minimize movement. She makes sacrifices by separating the bad eggs from good ones. With wisdom, she feeds the chickens first before feeding herself. She is responsible and protects the chicks from eagles and covers them from the cold with love and compassion.

Although you may be alone for a while, you can create your own flock. Always be diligent to know the flock's state. Give careful attention to your herds because there is a reason and a season for everything. When I talk of a flock, it can be the thing you do now—your business, studies, investments, savings, and work. When you take care of your flock, there will be plenty of goat meat and milk to feed your family and the lamb will provide you with clothing. We must work hard to produce more than we consume.

The characteristics of a hunter are quite different from those of a shepherd. A hunter consumes all he has gathered for a day and thinks of tomorrow, while a shepherd produces more than he or she consumes. Let's all take on the shepherd's character of producing more than we consume to always have more than we had in our daily lives.

The fact that we may not have parents or loved ones anymore doesn't mean that the world must end for us too. We still have life; we are still breathing. If nobody cares for you, so what? Care for yourself. Note that part of destiny is lonely. You can't mix everything up with everyone because we are all different. If you aren't different, you can't make a difference.

The best way to predict the future is by creating it today. Work hard, be assertive, connect to people globally, share your dreams and do new things every day.

As an orphan or someone in grief, keep yourself busy. Do anything that you can and ensure that on the daily or monthly basis you financially gain.

Keep good truck of the small beginning and with time, what you do shall become greater one day.

"Greatness is a small step taken many times."
Christina Goebel

Never lose hope, no matter how hard the situation can be. Things might not be working out for you but remind yourself of who you are and that afflictions are for a moment. Stay happy always and be positive, for happiness is the key to success.

"Well life for none of us has been a crystal stair, but we must keep moving, we must keep going. If you can't fly, run. If you can't run, walk. If you can't walk, crawl, but by all means, keep moving."
Martin Luther King, Jr.

Having hardships, sleeping without food, being rejected and feeling unloved did not make me unhappy, because I chose to be happy despite the challenges. I still connected with friends, shared my opinion, and built relationships with them. You've been given power to make your own decisions and no one can replace that. Everyone needs to build their own dream. The only thing is to start the process.

© 2019 George Omondi Owiti, "Coping with Loss"

Part Three

GoldenHeart

Chapter Twenty-Four
Using Your GoldenHeart

Feeling

I tell them I'm fine,
my feelings I hide.
Old people don't know
these feelings inside.

Overjoyed, then sad,
when will love grow?
Rollercoaster emotions
only young people know.

Is it just me?
Is it always like this?
Why can't there always
be happiness and bliss?

Guess that's called life.
I'll have to move on;
always be happy,
always be strong.

Share love with family,
neighbours and friends.
Feel love inside,
so it never ends.

Look to the future;
learn from the past.
Old minds and young hearts—
together at last.

That is your message:
don't feel alone;
enjoy all around you—
before long,
you're grown.

— babygo © *2019 BabyGo, "Feeling"*

When I was a teacher, one of the most common questions I heard was, "What is my purpose?" When my son asked me this, I said that he did not have to worry about finding the answer to that question. "Our purpose is to leave the world a better place," I said.

In the book, *GoldenHeart: How to Love Humanity*, I said, "Dear reader, please love the world as I love you. It will save you. It will save others. It will save our world."

A GoldenHeart is someone who looks for ways that they can be kind to others and help humanity. While it is wonderful to feed one person today, if we think of the bigger picture, we can feed more people with extra effort.

Imagine that it is winter, and you notice that people who are homeless are cold and hungry. Many areas provide hot soup for people who are homeless during the winter season because it meets two needs, food and warmth. If you cook soup for one person, could you extend that to soup for more? Yes, you could, and it would not cost much extra since you would add some more water and ingredients. What if you wanted to feed people across town? You could do many things to achieve this objective. You could unify local organizations who are focused in this area and increase the outreach through them. You could fundraise to provide more food. You could motivate strong leaders to develop local solutions. If you take it a step further, you can work together with people who are homeless to find housing solutions and jobs that they enjoy. This will empower them to change their lives for the better.

A creative mind solves problems. As you have seen, the world has tons of problems. I bet you never thought that you were one of the solutions! You have natural gifts and experiences that educated you. Beloved, your abilities and experiences have molded you into a problem solver for specific issues that are giving humanity trouble. Your abilities will increase as you grow older. The important part now is to be mindful that you may be the person to assist others in some areas. (Smile.)

How do you know which people need your help? Maybe the people in front of you are the ones that need you. Perhaps one day, you will create wonderful adoption processes, build a loving home for foster children, or design programs to enhance the foster care system. Young parents need support sometimes so that they can keep their children with them, and you could develop a program to do that.

To develop your GoldenHeart, spend more time watching what others need. Is anyone not eating? Have a conversation with him or her to learn why. Do any people around you have depressed expressions? Ask if they are feeling well or have a conversation with him or her. As you observe more people and ask them about their circumstances, you will see that people have similar problems.

When you encounter their troubles, ask yourself, "Why am I meeting these people with the same problem? How can I assist them?" You may not have the ability to support them today, but with time, you may have the opportunity to make a difference.

Not long ago, I went to a restaurant drive through and when we arrived at the window to pay, the cashier said that the person in front of us had paid for our bill. We did not know them, and they apparently had done this for no reason. The cashier at the window told us about the other driver's kindness with a delighted smile. I asked the cashier how much the person's bill was behind us. Since we could afford to pay for their bill, we did. This is not the first time I have heard about this type of gesture of good will for strangers.

Developing a habit of giving is an exercise for strengthening your GoldenHeart. I do believe this includes that you are generous with what you have, though many times, you may gift your help or things that you make for free. I have edited for other writers to encourage them to write and I publicize the work of others to show that what they say or do has value. Those things cost me nothing but my time. I wonder often why more people do not share their talents or promote the good work of others and it is possible that no one has suggested it to them. As I share this with you, Dearest Heart, I am eager for you to know the grand feeling of serving humanity.

One of my favorite things to do, though I do not plan it when it happens, is to make people cry with happiness. Have you seen this before? It often occurs when you surprise someone with an unexpected kindness that they feel is such a priceless treasure that it brings them to tears. They did not think anyone was paying attention to them, or that people cared about them that much. In some cases, they had a terrible day and then all of the sudden, you poured goodness into their life. Whatever was awful for them melts away and then they are left with relief, awe, and love.

If you pay close attention to others to see what they need, you will gain the ability to touch hearts in a memorable way. Though it takes time to develop the skill, it is worth the practice. We have the choice to give or to take, to love or to hate, to share kindness or shun it. When we give, we receive. When we love, we are loved. When we share kindness, the world returns the gesture. Giving, loving, and being kind also teaches us how to recognize when others gift us with these things. Many people do nice things that go unnoticed, but a person who cares for others regularly will often notice every tiny miracle that comes her or his way. By making generosity a part of your life, you bring abundance into it.

The world is not perfect, and we are no strangers to bad things. We have been deeply hurt by others—and we have also made mistakes. We have seen things that should not happen and have wished that the world could be a better place. When we think of the future, we think of what we can do today to create a brighter tomorrow for ourselves and others, but we also think of what others will do to improve the world and that is an exciting thing to consider.

Darling, you are like a bird. While in the nest, a baby bird only waits for adult birds to bring food. All those baby birds care about is food, ha ha! After a while, the babies realize that they have wings and that they might do something with them, so they flap their wings and—nothing happens! It is not the moment to fly. They have the desire, but the circumstances have not arrived. Still, they can eat like a bird and hang out with other baby birds in the nest. They are a bird; they just cannot fly yet.

One day, a baby bird ventures from the nest, spreads its wings, and suddenly, its wings catch the air and the baby bird rises upward into the sky. The wind pushes against its wings and it soars! Its view above the world is phenomenal. It sees light upon the waters and land, and people and cars look so tiny. It no longer worries about when its wings did not work, and it has no idea why the adult birds flew around and did things it could not do.

When the baby bird is older, it learns to fly higher and longer, faster and stronger, but more experienced birds amaze the former baby bird. And it wonders, when will I learn those fancy ways to fly? When will I learn to soar an inch over the water or turn sideways as I approach a mountain?

Finally, the baby bird learns those things too, and how to hunt worms quite well! Then, one day during a fancy spiral, the bird hears some baby birds chirping. It sees a parent nearby, struggling with a wing that has been damaged. It is unable to reach the nest. You realize that life is not about learning how to fly by yourself. It is learning how to fly with everyone else. So, you feed the babies and push the parent bird to a wider part of a tree branch so it can rest and heal.

The satisfaction that you had from flying and doing fancy spirals is nothing compared to that of ensuring that the baby birds ate. It did not matter that they were not your baby birds. They wanted to eat, and you had the desire to feed them. They needed love, and you had the desire to love them. When you found your gift of hunting worms and the ability to sense that you were needed and could fulfill that need, you became the bird you were meant to be. Your wings were never meant just to fly. They were meant to assist and save lives.

Dear GoldenHeart, this book is the beginning of your flight. With all the love we can deliver, we have written it so that you may fly and reach your destiny. For a while, you will have to trust us that you are needed by the world to do what only you can do. Eventually, Darling, you will fly and see the purpose behind your gifts and experiences. You will see that our faith in you was justified. You will make mistakes along the way, but do not dwell on those. Search for the moments when you can truly fly. You have joined our flock and you are welcome to it, forever. We are always here in these digital and physical pages for you, dear GoldenHeart, always and forever.

 # Anecdotes

Treasures Within

These things sight cannot see: a heart full of light, love, peace, integrity, fraternity, tolerance, unity, discipline, patience, faith, care, positivity and egalitarianism. When your heart is enriched with these heavenly elements, then it is a *Golden Heart*. No matter how much the world has wronged you, always share your golden heart with others. A pure, golden heart will help you to taste life's peaceful colours with an endless love.

We are blessed with life for a single time with thousands of opportunities.

Like a child can't learn to walk without falling, a person cannot learn something great without feeling pain and grievances. The Almighty has blessed us with several things and everything that comes in our life arrives for a reason— even pain.

Our blessings are not to make our lives easy, peaceful and contented, but to make use of our every breath to make this world better and happier.

It is great to aid others by providing food, shelter, and money, but their soul also needs attention. Souls can be satisfied and healed by caring, sharing, integrity, peace, support, true advice, honest feedback, guidance, encouragement, motivation, trust, and most importantly, with true love.

Do you know why many people fail to heal the soul? Whenever they feel pain or go through hard times, they always seek a way to get rid of those issues and never realize that this phase is more than suffering. When you take your pain into deep consideration and discover what it has been trying to teach you, only then will you end this pain forever by turning it into a healing ointment for others who are going through similar hardships.

A person gets several benefits from the soil by sowing seeds, growing crops, selling vegetables, fruits, lentils or grains, using mineral resources, selling or purchasing land and so on—but the same person is unable to find the treasures hidden beneath pain, hardships and suffering.

Prosperity cannot be harvested without trials and tribulations. No one has ever seen light without darkness, dreams without nightmares, friends without foes, beauty without pain, ease without hardships, results without exams, success without failures, hope without hopelessness or love without hate.

Is a seed's painful journey about being sown alone in the dark, waiting to grow into a plant, and from that into a tree? No! To beat the pain of darkness and be alone until turning into a plant and then into a tree is an exceptional act and struggle for a seed. People appreciate a seed for turning into a huge tree and call it success. But success is a process of growing up and moving forward—despite all the hardships and pain a seed faces alone. Success is defeating adversity on an individual level and ending your pain.

When a seed turns into a tree, that doesn't mean that its pain ends. The seed gains the ground by utilising patience, faith and persistence and defeating barriers and hardships—but that is still not its complete success.

Anything in the world can defeat trials and tribulations when it has turned its pain into a healing ointment for the wounds of others. Coming out of the soil and turning into a tree is an incredible act of inspiration by a seed, but you know what is more amazing? Providing fresh air, greenery, shade, flowers, fruits, fragrance and beauty for the world. In short, being fruitful for others. Overcoming your pain for yourself only is a great milestone, but what makes your victory complete is being fruitful for others after enduring difficult times. In order to remain fruitful for others, a seed must hold up the weight of a huge tree.

No matter how hard and harsh life becomes, remember that God has blessed you with your unique and special treasure. A seed cannot grow without being buried and success cannot be achieved without failure. Your special and unique treasure cannot be revealed without feeling, considering and learning from pain.

Even after being a kind soul, you will face people with harsh voices and dark visions. Never be afraid of them or call them bad without giving them some chances to show you the real them. Just as humans would never have known about the diamonds hidden in the coals mines if they had never explored the dark, sombre part of mines, human treasures are either hidden in the mines of traumas or beneath the soil of pain, hardships, wounds, trials and tribulations.

When you explore these mines or dig beneath the soil

intensely, then you will discover gold—your *Golden Heart.* Every treasure in this world decreases by giving, except two treasures. One is knowledge and the other one is a Golden Heart. Wherever you go, whomever you meet, don't forget to share your expanding treasures—your knowledge and your Golden Heart.

© *2019 Noorio Zehra, "Treasures Within"*

Only Love Can Bring Us Happiness

We live in a world which changes dramatically in many ways. For example, this summer has been very hot with temperatures over forty degrees Celsius in some countries. People have even died because of the heat. Our planet is in danger; what are we going to do about it? Still, we have a hard time facing it: climate change is a reality, the disrespect of the planet and one another. We are all responsible. Taking responsibility means doing what needs to be done and seeing the circumstances.

Our planet is dying, and we all need to realize this and change our lifestyles radically because it seems that we don't have much time left to do something about it. Without air and water, we can't survive; it's a gift of nature. We need to respect Mother Nature. We are blaming society, yet we are society. We are the ones that we have been waiting for, and the future is in our own hands. To make the world better, we need to change and that might not be easy. For example, time off the Internet is so important these days. Mental rest can improve productivity. Unplug and shut down a few times a day and embrace nature.

Also, society and families have changed. There's no such thing as "typical" anymore. The nuclear family has disappeared and with rising divorce rates and growing pressure in the workplace, parents are passing on childcare responsibilities to society, grandparents and other relatives. We are so focused on money that our relationships are not as important as our careers. But we are all free to make our own choices about what we want to focus on in our lives. Love is the most beautiful thing of your life, if you have it.

Love starts at home, and parenting is a lifelong commitment. If you don't love yourself, it's impossible to love another. A primary need is to love yourself—without that, you can't feel the love of others. A warm home is a home where there is love. The most important things in life are relationships—they are priceless. Compassion is an attitude based on the ability to be open-ended and warm-hearted. Caring is listening to another person's heart. Though compassion and caring are part of unconditional love, loving unconditionally doesn't mean you have to accept bad behavior. True love sets boundaries and guides us to do what's right.

If we can make the change from a consuming society to a needs-based one, some resources of nature can be left for the coming generations. Climate change isn't the problem. It's the climate in our hearts: if we loved, this wouldn't be happening. We need to do everything we possibly can to clean the oceans of plastic. We need to change this cruel world to a loving one, where people take care of each other and the planet. Always remember that your voice, compassion and kindness can help change—and save—the world.

The world lacks empathy, compassion, love and respect. That's why we need to learn how to love and respect ourselves first, and then others and our planet. Respecting others and being respected is a key component in living a happy life. Respect starts with respecting yourself. First, you need to be happy yourself. Happiness doesn't come from material things or money. It comes from loving and accepting yourself just the way you are. The first step to living a happier life is leaving the things you don't want behind.

What's the use of money if you haven't got happiness? What's the use of a big, fancy house if you haven't got a planet to put it on? You can't change the world by being part of majority. It's better to be poor and have wealth in your soul than to be rich with a heart of stone. We all need to take care of this planet and everything on it. As Mahatma Gandhi said, there's "enough for everyone's needs, but not for everyone's greed." If the wealth was evenly distributed, people could live and not fight for survival.

We must open our hearts and feel the love, empathy and compassion, because without love, we can't survive. Violence and terror attacks are signs of the lack of love; the world hungers for it. Love starts with you. We must love and respect ourselves—only then can the love spread to others. Words have a power that matters to our heart and soul. That is why we must choose our words wisely.

Motherhood is the authentic path of human experience during which we guide others towards awakening because mothers give birth and nurture their newborn infants. Mothers give life as Mother Earth does. That is why especially women can transmit good education to their children with love and further spread it in society.

Therefore, women need to value themselves as women and not compete with men about money and status, as it happens now. Strong motherhood is important in society: we need mothers who are selfless and loving and work hard to make sure their children are equipped with the knowledge, skills and abilities to make them competent human beings. They can be the symbol of love, trust and peace. Motherhood is the greatest possible investment for the future. Mothers are a special gift of God's Love sent to comfort and protect us always.

Fathers are as important as mothers; a child needs both parents. Strong fathers teach us the beauty of nature and the gentleness of our heavenly Father. John Wooden said, "The best gift a father can give his children is to love their mother." According to a popular quote by an anonymous author, our parents "hold our hand for a while and our heart forever." Do not worry if you don't have a mother or father; you can become a great mother or father when you listen to your heart and follow love. You just have to show that you genuinely care. Everyone can change her or his life with the power of Love and forgiveness.

© 2019 Jaana Uolamo, "Only Love Can Bring Us Happiness"

Kindness: An Attitude of Gratitude

One morning whilst I was on the train, the conductor came through checking tickets. There was this young boy sitting opposite myself and a friend who did not have a ticket. The conductor asked him where he going and what station he got on at, and he told conductor he did not have a ticket. The conductor then proceeded to give him a fine, but this kind lady stepped in and paid for the ticket. She said she did it because this could have been her son, and she would like to know that there are people out there who are willing to help others. The young boy was so happy that he couldn't stop thanking the woman. It was such a kind thing to do, and kindness really does speak volumes. When we are kind to others, this creates a ripple effect. Everyone can be kind to one person and all over the world, those who need help will receive help from someone. Kindness is such a simple thing and yet it's the most important to those who need it. We can make a difference in someone's life if we try—one person at a time.

I helped an older gentleman a week ago who needed to cross a busy road to do some shopping. He was standing on the crossing, but no one stopped for him to cross. I asked him whether he would like me to help him cross. He said yes, and I took hold of his hands and helped him cross over. He thanked me, saying he was going to be okay, but I doubted that. He seemed frail and weak. I wished I could have done more and wondered why he was out in the first place. It's probably because he had no one to help him, which is very sad. It's a blessing to look after our parents and elders and to help those who once cared for us, since we will grow old one day and may need someone to help us. We should use every opportunity to care for our loved ones, even if it a simple phone call, because after they are gone, it's too late to help.

When I look around, there are many that need help. Life is strange, with lots of twists, turns, and corners, and uphill and downhill trips. When you are downhill, it must be a devastating place. I always say to others, "Please do not distress yourself. Be happy, have faith and trust in God." Lend a helping hand to others. You never know when you will need someone's help. Be kind, considerate and compassionate toward others; love and accept them for who they are. Loving others is not "I love you;" it's more about having a love for humanity. Give without expecting anything in return. This is a true golden heart, to be able to give without receiving.

Develop an attitude of gratitude and live a life that has meaning. We live in a beautiful world full of lovely places and things, but sometimes all someone wants is to be happy and to enjoy the little things in life, such as visiting family and friends, spending time chatting, or helping other to do things that need to get done. Work with others to empower them to live happy, satisfying and more enriched lives. Life is difficult and we all have different journeys and paths to take. Many of us have been hurt and have lost loved ones and have suffered some setbacks, but life goes on regardless of the situation. We all have a story to tell and dreams to accomplish. Sadly, some people's dreams and stories are never told. Help others to complete their stories and share them with the world.

© 2019 Kamla Peerbocus, "Kindness: An Attitude of Gratitude"

Kindness, the World and You

I grew up as the youngest of nine cousins. All of us lived in the same house and were raised by my grandmother, seventy-six miles away from Beijing. Growing up as the only girl, my grandmother always made sure I grew up strong. She showed me how we can love the world with an open heart in a difficult environment; I oftentimes went to bed feeling hungry and never had an opportunity to drink milk or have any treats. When my grandma passed away twelve years ago, she called me to her bedside. Her last few words were: "Stay special. Make the world proud. Spread my ashes at a tall mountain."

Going to Grandma's funeral was the defining moment of my life. There, I realized what she meant by "being special with a kind heart." So many people showed up at her funeral. Many of them had never met Grandma. They had heard about her selflessness and how she never stopped helping others when they were in need.

A little boy came up to me at the funeral and handed over his drawing of Grandma. It was a piece of bread, wrapped up in a napkin. He said, "That piece of bread was given to me by Grandma and it saved me from fainting on a cold winter evening." That evening, I listened to so many stories about the positive impact Grandma made on others. She had never mentioned a word about any of her good works.

Right then and there, I determined to carry on Grandma's legacy and use my Golden Heart to help others.

So how do you love the world? To love the world, you need to love yourself first. Having self-esteem is the foundation for you to love and be loved. Having grown up with an empty stomach oftentimes, Grandma taught us what's really important in life. She created a safe environment for us to take the risk of making our own decisions and allowed us to learn from our mistakes. She helped us understand that there was a consequence for every decision we made. It is often said that one needs to lose a battle in order to win the war. There is no need to feel defeated if you lost a battle. I finally realized the real meaning behind these words, and I share it with you now, Dear One: don't ever, ever give up.

Secondly, to love is to give without expecting anything in return. I waited tables at a restaurant during my college days in Ithaca, New York. Working seven evenings a week and going to school during the day deteriorated my health. One evening, I started coughing and blood came out with my cough. I decided not to take that night off, even though I really needed to go home. That happened to be the busiest night ever. Customers lined up to visit the Chinese buffet restaurant I worked at.

All I remember from that night was that I fainted. When I woke up in the emergency room at the local hospital, flowers were on the table with an envelope. A handwritten note said: "Helen, here is a token of appreciation for what you have done for us in the past months. Your hospital bill has been taken care of. Rest and get well." The envelope was filled with dollar bills worth my whole week's pay. My eyes were full of tears. That was a defining moment for me. I realized how much of a positive impact we can make on the lives of others.

So how do we inspire others to love the world? We can all play a part with random acts of kindness or being part of a community to help others. I encourage you to think about what legacy you'd like to leave behind. In other words, how would you like to be remembered by others? Here is how I'd like to be remembered: Passion, Curiosity and Grit. My passion for having a Golden Heart leads to my Curiosity for finding ways to help others. Grit means that I will overcome obstacles no matter how challenging life might be.

When you know what you stand for and what you want to be remembered for, you can then look for opportunities to live up to your promise. Understanding what you want to leave behind is a major milestone of your Golden Heart journey.

Dear Ones, we are always here and will always be part of your journey. Remember, there is a happy ending if you choose it to be so. It is not the end yet if it is not happy. Take time and energy to explore, love and be loved with your Golden Heart.

© 2019 Helen Yu, "Kindness, the World and You"

Where There Is Love . . . There You Are

Dear Golden Heart,

I want you to imagine for a moment that you are now entering a safe place. A familiar place. A place where you are free to be yourself. A place where you can connect with your heart and feel the ultimate love that created you.

As your imagination takes off, let your heart soar. At first, you may be afraid of this place or even feel like it is elusive or unreachable. Keep going back to this place. Each day, take a few peaceful moments to imagine this safe place that is filled with love.

This place belongs to you and as time goes on, you will become aware that you have been in this safe place the whole time. There will come a moment that a knowing will wash over you—all along, your heart has waited for you to see how incredibly divine you are. In this place, you have found your Soul.

You're home.

Love is where you belong.

When people talk to you about changing the world, the idea can seem utopian. Living your truth, following your heart and spreading love and kindness everywhere you tread is all you need to do. To spread love in the world, you need to first honour your own heart. Nurture the pain you feel and connect with the inherent beauty within the depths of your soul. It is there; keep searching.

Your journey may not have been easy. It may have been downright hard. And for that I am sorry. I wish that I could wrap you up in an ineffable ball of love. Know that energetically, I am. Through these words, we are connected by an invisible thread of love. If you need help, please don't be afraid to draw from it.

It is an unconditional love that binds us all.

Within you, strength and courage are hidden under pain. A pain that you deserve to have, and that you need to honour and nurture. Your individual blueprint is unique. You have a unique set of circumstances and your soul is full of a wisdom that very few people have—a knowing of the power of compassion and kindness that is needed to aid someone on their journey.

Now that you know that you have infinite love inside of you, please share it. Contrary to popular opinion, love is not just romance.

Divine love is:

- Kindness,
- Prayer,
- Gratitude,
- Compassion, and
- Forgiveness.

You have the power to be a beacon of love. Use your past as the container that holds the wisdom that you shine.

Every day, when you enter the big, bright world, do it with pride. Do it with kindness and remember to include self-appreciation. Your own heart is worthy of the love and compassion that you send into the world. Your soul believes in your strength. It will pick you up, always. This is not to say the road ahead will be easy but allow love and kindness to give you the strength to face the many speed bumps life will throw your way.

Some people go their whole lives not seeing how beautiful their soul is. Your life is just beginning. You have so much potential for love and kindness. Don't be afraid to use it. Regardless of your beliefs or religion, you are encased in love every step of the way. There is nothing needed from you. Love just is. Share this love, so that when other people are down, you can light the path ahead for them. There is great joy that comes from shining your light on another's journey.

When you shine your light on others, you heal your own heart. In a pure act of giving, you become one with another soul. The connection is palpable, and it gives life so much meaning.

I love you. I don't need to know you to love you. We are all a part of the same family. The human family.

Be love.

© 2019 Kylie Riordan, "Where There Is Love . . . There You Are"

Golden Hearts to Be

When your heart is a star,
when your sadness goes so far—
know one thing:

the Divine gave you wings
to fly high
above any sigh.

You are blessed.
Be an oddity
with your difference.
Create happiness above substance.
Collect hearts;
let them create art.
Put kindness inside love,
your brand like a pretty dove.

You are human.
Love is your fan and
comes to you everywhere
when you need to share
the GoldenHearts
making them a part.

Let people ask
the meaning of GoldenHearts.
Answer them with pride.
"It's the hearts I found
after suffering, struggling and expressing
how to lose nearly everything
and turn it into gain.
It's the meaning of existing;
it's life inside persisting."
I will preserve it until the end.

That's my aim, dear friends.

It Is You

My wish for you, my Dearest, Most Precious Angelic One,
is to live a life of endearment from the rise and set of
every sun,
to love the world around you, all things,
like:

the chubby pugs,
hot cocoa in steaming mugs,
the butterflies on milkweed in May,
the D+ you thought was an A,
the first kiss,
the ball you swung at and missed,
the last mile of a race,
the no-ice cream days,
the thousand-legged bug that crawled into your shoe,
the horrible day you'd like to redo,
the swim at the lake,
the first-quarter-in-the-football-game ankle break,
the times you make a friend laugh,

the song you sang, and everyone clapped,
the beautiful person you stare at
in the mirror, every morning, every night.
Love the world for all its brokenness and beauty.
God made one perfect gift for the world to see;
it is you.

From the beginning of time,
it always has been
loving the world
is
loving you.
I can tell you only what I believe to be true—
and I believe in you.

@ 2019 Michele Kelly, "It Is You"

About This Book

One day, I was listening to The Beatles' *1* compilation and the song "Let It Be" played. I remembered reading an article years ago that said that the Mother Mary mentioned in that song as coming to the narrator "in times of trouble" was a reference to lyricist Sir Paul McCartney's mother.

After she died, the article said, McCartney's mother would appear to him when he needed someone. Since I have a son, I wanted to be there for him when I am no longer on Earth. If I wrote a book for him about life, then he would have a piece of me and hear my voice when he feels alone and needs compassion and hope. You see, I don't want to miss those times he needs me, just because I go to Heaven. So, I decided to put a piece of Heaven in a book. I guess you can say it's Paul McCartney's fault. (Wink.)

I don't know how many times I played "Let It Be" in the car while I drove and thought about the life lessons needed for a forever companion and love inspiration manual for my son. I had previously been inspired to write *GoldenHeart: How to Love Humanity* for my son and the world to have a way to achieve their full potential in love. But *GoldenHeart II* had a different purpose—to speak to my son when he misses my company, long after I'm gone.

When I thought I had the perfect concept, "Let It Be" continued to play and I thought, What about all the people who don't have a Mother Mary like Sir Paul and I have? Who will be there for them during their time of need? I played the song many times, each time thinking about how I could solve that problem.

Like Sir Paul McCartney and The Beatles loved people with their music—all the Eleanor Rigbys, Father McKenzies, and Nowhere Men—I wanted to love people and be there for every orphan, foster child, foundling, bereaved adult—and for all the world's lonely people. I cried because, of course, I can't be there for everyone. Not in person. And I simply couldn't *let that be!*

But I can be there for everyone in a book!

So, I wrote down the topics I wanted to share with my son and you so that for the rest of your lives, you can consult the book whenever you need guidance or a loving voice. I wrote my learned lessons for each section.

I quickly understood that my advice isn't enough, but also that the love I have for the world isn't enough. My words don't reach every heart. Therefore, I needed to find the most loving people I could and invite them to write for you, knowing that if I can't reach your heart—one of them can.

The authors here are people I deeply admire. They aren't afraid to love people. Somehow, life taught them the beauty of loving humanity and many of them share that love daily at home, in their communities and businesses, and in social media. None of us are perfect people—don't think that for a minute! We would all laugh with you if you thought we were perfect. But we are a few of the many people who discovered how to love the people of the world.

For every dark and sinister being, there are more loving

ones. While some people give up because of their troubled pasts, many become stronger and more beautiful because of their pain.

There is no greater power in the world than the daily expression of love, kindness, and compassion. Use them. Find out for yourself.

If you read this far, you know what pain and loss are. You know disappointment. You know fear. You have been so lonely and have felt that you don't belong. Some people are hard to reach and seem so picky about who they accept as their friends.

Don't let suffering separate you from the wonder and amazing presence that you are. I want to give you the best reason ever not to give up or be less than your best self. Because a whole bunch of strangers from across the world got together to become your family so that you will never be alone. We took a stand against all the negative elements out there and wrote with our hearts to you. Some of us cried while we wrote for you and cried while we read what others of us shared. Some of us laughed at our silly thoughts. Others of us shared searingly painful things that happened to us to bring light to your life. Poets crafted poems for you! We opened ourselves in vulnerability, just like family does. If making yourself vulnerable to others isn't love, I don't know what is!

Not only that, but we all agreed that you would have this in digital format for free! We don't care about the money.

We care about YOU.

Since you know that this group of people loves you, then you can go out there and spread that love. No matter what happens, keep your kindness, your compassion, your talents, your skills, your faith, and your heart whole. Let no one separate you from all the love you can give.

When life gets impossible, come to us. We will surround you with love. You will gain strength from us and for the rest of your life, you will know without doubt that you will never, ever be alone again.

We put it in writing.

We are your family.

May every day of your life be blessed, and may you bless the world every day you live.

~Christina Goebel and the GoldenHearts

@lovegoldenheart on Twitter & #GoldenHearts

www.lovegoldenheart.com

"Illuminate yourself in your surroundings, with the golden glow from within, friends."

Pratosh Vashi, 2019 tweet

Teaser

If you enjoyed *GoldenHeart II: We Are Your Family*, read the inspiration love manual that inspired it, *GoldenHeart: How to Love Humanity*, by Christina Goebel, for sale at online bookstores worldwide in e-book and in print. Here's an excerpt:

"Everyone who has ever done a kind deed for us, or spoken one word of encouragement to us, has entered into the make-up of our character and of our thoughts, as well as our success."
George Matthew Adams

I'm convinced that there are no better people, nothing closer to our concept of human angels, than those who make it their mission to improve the world. Whether their actions are large or small is not relevant. A great person needs only walk down the street to make a difference, by releasing the bonds of others, freeing them from poverty, embracing them during crises, and advocating for them when they do not have the resources, opportunity, or voice.

Thankfully, such people have existed, now exist, and will exist. Such names listed here in this book are some who might inspire us to fly in the direction of distress, poverty, and injustice, and help others to soar above it and take their wings.

In June of 2007 on PBS' *Nature*, I was moved by a Frederic Lilien documentary about a light-colored, red-tail hawk, Pale Male, who resided

in New York City's Central Park. No other red-tail hawk had lived there before him: he was the first. After a while, he attracted a mate, and they eventually had offspring. One day, crows attacked their nest, and the mother remained with their young while Pale Male alone defended his family. He was greatly outnumbered but succeeded in securing their safety. Because of his sacrifice, his young survived.[1]

If we think we aren't defenders, we sell ourselves short. The most honorable thinking that we can pursue is that which adopts the world as our nest, and all people as our offspring. When they are prepared to take flight, we do not fly for them but assist them in their efforts to learn how to take to wing. We share a wing, a meal, fend off predators, or secure a perch. Perhaps we don't sail as gossamer-winged angels, but this is the truth of human flight: we walk on the ground, but our minds soar.

Maybe you've seen concentric circles. One circle inside of another. They don't touch, yet because one circle is inside of the other, they're related. Perhaps you've also seen birds fly in circles. One of us must first take to the sky and set the path for the first circular flight pattern. I say a circular flight because we must be aware of what is happening by carefully inspecting the ground, not by flying away from where we've been or congregating in the park awaiting feed. Following our pattern, others will fly around us in concentric circles.

With one angel, an endless number of angels may fly around them. Mahatma Gandhi set an example with nonviolent protests and inspired other angels, such as Cesar Chavez, against civil injustices in America, and the Dalai Lama in favor of Tibet. We cannot count how many lives have been improved by their fearless flight.

We are not all politicians and whether we will be should not burden us now. What matters is that when the opportunity presents, when we discover someone's flight hindered, we take to the air. We assist; we facilitate; we defend. Our flight pattern is a concentric circle, and others follow.

I leave this book as a gift to the world in more than one way. First, it is an encouragement to those who have already taken flight to show us the way to reduce world suffering and assist those in need. Second, it is a flight pattern for those who haven't yet taken wing to make a difference in the world. Third, it is a legacy for my son, perhaps some of my students who I've taken under wing, and everyone everywhere.

As a legacy, my book takes flight as a first circle, to be followed by more. Each circle will increase in size. My son's humanitarian flight, for example, will hopefully exceed mine, and those who receive his legacy will overshadow him, and so on until significant progress is made and a whole species of kindness pervades the world.

May this inspire everyone to start a species of kindness in foreign places, on distant shores, in neglected corners, and especially in those areas where we have been blind, our nests. We each need to gather our young, or if we lack that, the young of others, and set a flight pattern, so that one day, we back away and rest in the magnificence, beauty, depth, and truth of humanitarian endeavors taking wing!

May we all be lovers of Humanity.

"Man is a living duty, a depository of powers that he must not leave in a brute state. Man is a wing."
José Martí

Golden*Heart*

HOW TO LOVE HUMANITY

Christina Goebel

**Learn more at
www.lovegoldenheart.com**

---

1. Janet Hess, *Pale Male*, Nature, Directed by Frederic Lilien (New York, NY: FL Productions Corporation, 2004).

Another of Christina Goebel's Books with Love

The GoldenHeart and BirthRight series examine the depths of love and compassion, faith and personal courage in different ways.

The BirthRight dystopian science fiction epic fantasy series pits the worst of technology against the best of humanity, exploring the full scope of human compassion and sacrifice. We can have a better future if we plan for it.

"Christina Goebel does a fine job of capturing the human elements left in this futuristic society, from the politics of survival to the psychology of love:
'This woman must be in his future, if not in the stars, then in a destiny he will carve from hewn rock…'"

MIDWEST BOOK REVIEW D. Donovan, Senior Reviewer

"The author developed a storyline that show the sacrifices needed to make a better world by weaving together romance, adventure, terror with some humour to create a great story."

Amazon review

* * *

"A brilliant start to the series..."
"A mixture of science fiction and high fantasy, Birth Right keeps readers engrossed with its interesting premise, intriguing plot, and compelling narrative ... Fans will eagerly await for the next installment."

PRAIRIES BOOK REVIEW

* * *

"This would make a great movie!"
"Through heart and fruition, destinies come together along this spiral of a journey."

Amazon verified purchase

* * *

"'99 feels a chill, too. She has decided what she must do.' I read that part and thought NOOOO YOU HAVE NO IDEA GIRL, YOU HAVE NO IDEA!!!" "The final fight scene was so emotional and suspenseful, it was such an enjoyable read…" **"I really held my breath for several pages …"** "Being a SCI FI book, I didn't expect comedy, so I was glad that many pages throughout the book made me giggle."

Amazon review

* * *

"Christina wove together a wonderful storyline that was **hard to put down!"**

Amazon review

* * *

"I loved this story and it scared me to death. But wow, it could happen or could it? **Awesome read!"**

Amazon review

* * *

In the illustrated dystopian epic fantasy *Birth Right: Galak's Rising*, Galak, a cruel cyborg obsessed with creating a race of superior beings, demands that Valki twins compete for a Birthright.

The courage of two young women to resist Galak's law pits princes, kings, and mighty warriors against a merciless foe.

Art by Kent Burles

BIRTHRIGHT: GALAK'S RISING,
the first of the BIRTHRIGHT trilogy.

CPSIA information can be obtained
at www.ICGtesting.com
Printed in the USA
BVHW040157150521
607271BV00001B/81

9 781087 961088